From Ignorance to
Bliss

God's Heart Revealed
through Down Syndrome

ENDORSEMENTS

A very personal and enlightening narrative of how God can take a challenge like Down syndrome and use it to bless and encourage people across the globe. Read how Annie and Jeff Yorty's daughter Alyssa, born with Down syndrome, is drawn to touch people with the gospel of Jesus here at home and even in Siberia.
—**Josh D. McDowell**, author

You can feel the heart, passion and never-ending faith in this uplifting, soul-nourishing novel. As a mother of a daughter with Down syndrome, the line I loved most was, "I knew Alyssa was a gift from God created according to His exact specifications. I knew He made no mistakes." Annie is so right! I truly believe that our kids are sent here for a purpose: to teach, to love, and to make the world a better place! I feel so blessed to be surrounded by their incredible spirit everyday which is why I so appreciate Annie sharing that love in this book. Annie, I really think your message will take people from ignorance to understanding, as happened to you! Thank you for acting on your message to yourself 25 years ago!
—**Nancy Gianni**, Founder and Chief Belief Officer, GiGi's Playhouse Down Syndrome Achievement Centers

There are times in our lives when something unexpected occurs to completely change what we thought our lives would be. This happened to Annie Yorty and her husband when they received the news that their daughter, Alyssa, was born with Down syndrome. In her book, *From Ignorance to Bliss*, Annie shares their story — the challenges, the surprises, the disappointments, the accomplishments, and the lessons learned about love, family, and God's ultimate faithfulness. In a world where children with disabilities are too often discarded, rejected, institutionalized, or abandoned, this is a story of a couple who courageously embraced the gift of their daughter with Down syndrome and by God's grace, raised a remarkable young lady who is making a difference in the world.

—**Dr. Craig von Buseck**, Director of Digital Content, FocusontheFamily.com

From Ignorance to Bliss: God's Heart Revealed through Down Syndrome is a beautiful and inspiring read. The book is vivid proof that our perfect God does not make a single mistake. Each of His children are perfectly designed to carry out and fulfill the mission He created us for.

Annie Yorty is transparent in sharing the struggles encountered through the journey of Down syndrome. However, she eloquently pens the triumphs and victories that unequivocally supersede every single hardship.

Each chapter details the relentless love of a mother, and the determination of an extraordinary young lady who is fearless in reaching her goals. More importantly, every story is a brilliant reflection of God's perfect, undeniable love.

As the mother of an incredible son with Down syndrome, I can personally relate with many accounts in this book. As the mother of two typical children (who are equally as incredible), many of the stories strongly resonate with me.

As human beings, we will inevitably encounter circumstances that incite fear, break our hearts, and leave us begging for answers. These things are not exclusive to families who have a loved one with a disability. However, in every situation, we have a God who has perfectly mapped out our lives and generously granted us with the tools to navigate our paths. *From Ignorance to Bliss: God's Heart*

Revealed through Down Syndrome is the perfect reminder of the love He has for His children.
—**Michelle Norwood**, *A Little Something Extra Ice Cream*

Annie's story is wonderfully relatable. She puts into words what so many of us experience—that not just homeschooling, but all of life gives us opportunities to believe in the faithfulness of God and allow Him to shape and grow us into who He desires us to be. Through her story, Annie lets us know we're not the only one who struggles with God's plan for us. She also shows how God's perspective, ways, and thoughts are better than ours, perfect for us, and life changing when we release our ways for His.
—**Ginger Wayde**, Christian Homeschool Association of Pennsylvania board and host of *Chattin' with CHAP*

Annie Yorty has the patience of Job, the wisdom of Solomon, and the courage of the Apostle Paul. She knew how to "wait upon the Lord" when her daughter Alyssa was born. Alyssa has Down syndrome. In this well-written book, the life-changing journey for Annie's family is detailed with honesty, poignancy, and ultimate triumph.

Although Annie was asked to undergo a special test to see if there was something in her pregnancy that might be of concern, she declined the suggestion and waited on the birth of her child. "I truly never gave another thought to the possibility there could be a problem with our expected baby," she writes. She now knows that "Alyssa was the soil conditioner used to awaken the seed of faith that had long ago buried in my heart."

The day of Alyssa's birth is described with humility and grace. Annie's husband Jeff was always close by. They shared the joy of parenthood. They knew of the challenges that lay ahead. But, there—in the delivery room—"we bowed our heads together, and Jeff prayed over Alyssa."

From Ignorance to Bliss: God's Heart Revealed through Down Syndrome is inspiring reading. The nonprofit organization I have headed since 1983—The Baptist Children's Homes of North Carolina—operates nine Homes for youth/adults like Alyssa. I know first-hand the joy that our residents bring to those who have the privilege and opportunity to know them.

Read this book with the Bible close by. Annie provides Scripture references which you will want to read and re-read. You will, indeed, see "God's Heart Revealed" in this book. Thank you, Annie Yorty, for leading us on this journey *From Ignorance to Bliss.*

—Dr. Michael Blackwell, President/CEO, Baptist Children's Homes of North Carolina, www.bchfamily.org

I've had the opportunity to review *From Ignorance to Bliss: God's Heart Revealed through Down Syndrome* by Annie and Alyssa Yorty. Guided by their faith and determination Annie and Alyssa came to me in search of hope and answers. In time, both wishes were realized, as Alyssa responded nicely to medication, counseling, and His grace. In making their journey, Alyssa and her family were transformed into a stronger, wiser, and more loving version of their prior selves. Truly inspiring and worthy of celebration! Amen.

—Dr. George Capone, Director of Down Syndrome Clinic and Research Center, Kennedy Krieger Institute

Without a doubt, Annie Yorty is a voice to be listened to as she openly and honestly shares from the depths of her heart concerning her lifelong journey with her Down syndrome daughter. *From Ignorance to Bliss: God's Heart Revealed through Down Syndrome*, clearly and practically lays out what this life might look like and helps us be filled with hope that will inspire any parent, grandparent, or family member who finds themselves in this similar situation. This book reminds us that with God, all things are possible.

—**Toby Hopper**, full-time missionary with Global Training Network

I met Annie and Alyssa through a community group for families, caregivers and individuals who have special needs called BLAST. I had seen them at church a few times, but our lives had not crossed paths much previously. Being an Autism Support teacher in the Waynesboro Area School District for over twenty years, I have connections with many families in our community whose children have special needs, and we know some of the same people, but due to Alyssa's age, I had missed out on this relationship until recently.

I was honored when Annie asked me to read her book, *From Ignorance to Bliss*, and was captivated from the first moment. It is beautifully written, easy to read, and continually points the reader to Christ. I felt the pain, joy, fear, excitement, and loneliness in each chapter. I moved through her journey of life with Alyssa with God, with each turn of the page. Annie's imagery is delightful and the verses she chose to tie into each step of the journey are quite insightful.

Everyone who reads Annie's book will either understand and empathize as they have walked a similar path, or be amazed by the difficult yet rewarding steps God took them through. Either way, you are in for a blessing!

—**Laura Richardson**, Autism Support Teacher

From Ignorance to
Bliss

God's Heart Revealed
through Down Syndrome

Annie Yorty

ELK LAKE PUBLISHING INC.

PUBLISHING THE POSITIVE
Plymouth, Massachusetts

A Christian Company
ElkLakePublishingInc.com

COPYRIGHT NOTICE

Cover: Lana Ziegler, Derinda Babcock
Interior Design: Deb Haggerty
Editor(s): Carol McClain, Deb Haggerty

PUBLISHED BY: Elk Lake Publishing, Inc., 35 Dogwood Drive, Plymouth, MA 02360, 2023

Library Cataloging Data

Names: Yorty, Annie and Yorty, Alyssa (Annie Yorty and Alyssa Yorty)

From Ignorance to Bliss: God's Heart Revealed through Down Syndrome / Annie Yorty and Alyssa Yorty

194 p. 23cm × 15cm (9in × 6 in.)

ISBN-13: 978-1-64949-836-6 (paperback) | 978-1-64949-837-3 (trade hardcover) | 978-1-64949-838-0 (trade paperback) | 978-1-64949-839-7 (e-book)

Key Words: Inspirational memoir; Down syndrome; parenting child with disabilities; autobiography; Christian living nonfiction; special needs children; parenting a special needs child

Library of Congress Control Number: 2023935225 Nonfiction

DEDICATION

I must, of course, dedicate this book to its subject, my dear Alyssa Susie Q, my sweet potato and best girl, along with my amazing Father who entrusted her to me. I also cannot forget my partner in crazy, Jeff, who laughs and loves along with me on this journey from ignorance to bliss.

TABLE OF CONTENTS

ACKNOWLEDGMENTS

Since Father God originates every good thing from above (James 1:17), I acknowledge my inability to pen *From Ignorance to Bliss* on my own. I asked him to discard every word that might not represent him well and allow only his message to be told. His constant goodness provided the inspiration to write the story he's been writing on my heart for decades.

I am forever grateful to my husband, Jeff, who, when the time was right, reminded me of a scrap of paper with three words—"ignorance is bliss"—I had thrown into a drawer twenty-five years earlier. His prodding motivated me to begin.

I credit writing partners Lisé Buell and Shirley Mozena, and mentors Katy Kauffman and Beebee Kauffman from Lighthouse Bible Studies for helping me hone my writing skills and accommodating a gazillion questions.

When I chatted with a kind, older gentleman named Les Stobbe at lunch one day at a writers conference, I never guessed he would advocate for *Ignorance is Bliss* with Elk Lake Publishing a week later. I praise God for Les and for Deb Haggerty, who saw potential and took a chance on a newcomer.

I also want to recognize and appreciate Carol McClain and Joyce Erickson for their editing skills and encouragement which exponentially improved the finished product.

Too many to name have influenced me to grow in grace as a mother and as a daughter of my heavenly Father. God sees their diligence, and I pray he showers them with blessings.

Finally, the love of my family adds immeasurable joy to my life. Without them I wouldn't have this story to tell. Jeff, Alyssa, Stuart, and Joy are almost always eager to give me a cuddle whenever I need one. Their support keeps me going through all the twists and turns of life.

INTRODUCTION

About five years into my journey as Alyssa's mom, a thought popped into my head. *I'm so glad I didn't know all that was coming down the pike when Alyssa was first born.* If I had possessed even an inkling of what I would face, I'm sure my heart would have fainted within me. But my ignorance bolstered the courage I needed to face each new obstacle. A sort of bliss, one might say.

The idea for *From Ignorance to Bliss: God's Heart Revealed through Down Syndrome* took root in my heart. I scrawled a few words on a sticky note and tossed it into a drawer for later. For the right time.

I did not dream decades would pass before I wrote about my journey with God from spiritual ignorance to blissfully knowing him. Life hit hard in the intervening years. I wondered when, and sometimes if, the book would come to fruition. Over time, the idea never left my mind as God taught me, as he prepared me to share this message by assigning me to his holy classroom at Jesus's feet.

For some, sitting at the feet of Jesus to receive his wisdom comes naturally, but that's not my story. I needed to be prodded a bit—well, really, a lot—to assume a humble position.

My kids, especially Alyssa, have strong wills. I have always told them they come by the trait honestly. When they tested my motherly resolve, I assured them, though their wills are strong, mine had been honed by many more years of conditioning than theirs. Funny how my resolve never deterred them from competing for first place.

"Strong will" is a nicer way of saying stubborn. Maybe even prideful.

I admit I've been stubborn through and through. I've clung to my own foolish ideas to the bitter end before admitting God had a better plan. So though I pursue lifelong learning, I have also acted like a know-it-all at times. God has his work cut out for him when he wants to turn my head in a new direction, to see things his way instead of my way. I'm not at all implying he's not up to the challenge. God's will is, hands down, strongest of all. His will is perfect—infused by the wisdom of his omniscience.

All this true confession shows I more than most perhaps, needed a push—something cataclysmic—to make me drop and learn at the feet of Jesus. When my first knee-buckling experience happened, I was a twenty-five-year-old wayward and ignorant young wife with a newborn baby girl embarking on a journey into an unknown world of Down syndrome.

The definition of ignorance is simple—lacking knowledge. Lack of knowledge alone should not be considered derogatory. No one possesses understanding about all subjects, so everyone may be deemed at least somewhat ignorant. Still, the word conjures a negative connotation. Nevertheless, as a young mom, I claimed this characteristic for myself. I maintain to this day ignorance about what would come was good for me.

Thomas Gray coined the term "ignorance is bliss" in his 1742 poem, "Ode on a Distant Prospect of Eton College." He argued we achieve a state of happiness—bliss—by being ignorant of certain facts. Though we perversely pursue complete knowledge to be like God, human beings lack the resources to bear its heavy burden. Because the weight of omniscience would crush us, we must strike a balance between ignorance and knowledge. As a child of God, I see my ignorance as a void to be filled at the right time by the right Person.

Blissful ignorance is good—until it's not. Eventually, we need to acquire knowledge so we may choose appropriate and wise action. Received at the right time and in the right dose, knowledge helps us adjust our course to accommodate a new reality. "Your word is a lamp to my feet and a light to my path" (Psalm 119:105). This Bible verse suggests God doesn't point a glaring floodlight across our entire future. He illuminates only our next few steps. If not, we'd stumble across small roots and branches underfoot as we gape at jagged peaks looming ahead.

Instead, God holds my hand, guiding me along my journey in life with Alyssa, one step at a time. He draws my attention to the beautiful scenery when my eyes are downcast. He points out the road signs with information and warnings. When I'm thirsty for understanding, he doesn't release the fire hydrant of his vast knowledge and expect me to gulp from a raging flow. Instead, he offers me a sip from his infinite well of wisdom. His supply provides the precise amount for the moment. God equips me with enough for each day he's planned. Enough to keep a balance between ignorant bliss and overwhelming knowledge.

What follows is a scrapbook of ignorance-busting lessons I've learned from God through Alyssa. They are not comprehensive or final. I've chosen to include snapshots which tweaked my thinking and sometimes refocused my worldview. God used these experiences to reorient the way I perceive him, others, and myself. I hope to provide an accurate, transparent glimpse through the window of the life of one person with Down syndrome—the good, the bad, and the ornery—without sugarcoating or overdramatizing. Though she is a unique individual, I hope others will glean tidbits of insight from her experiences.

This approach will appeal to those in the broader disability community as well as those who desire to better understand people with intellectual differences. Experience with Down syndrome, however, is not required to appreciate God's eternal and universal truths I've discovered through parenting Alyssa. No doubt those who have never delighted in knowing one created with an extra twenty-third chromosome will also find they can relate to our joys and struggles because they span all spectrums of life.

I base my overarching goal for sharing life with Alyssa in such a personal way upon these verses:

> What was from the beginning, what we have heard, what we have seen with our eyes, what we have looked at and touched with our hands, concerning the Word of Life—and the life was manifested, and we have seen and testify and proclaim to you the eternal life, which was with the Father and was manifested to us ... Indeed our fellowship is with the Father, and with His Son Jesus Christ. These things we write, so that our joy may be made complete. (1 John 1:1–2)

God compels me to tell what I have seen, and yes, what I have touched through my experiences concerning the Word of Life. My journey from ignorance to bliss is really God's magnificent story working through our beautiful, yet messy, lives. I hope you find my retelling to be interesting, informative, humorous, and poignant (though probably not all at the same time).

As you read, I pray your eyes are opened to the God of the universe who created you and wants you to know him.

WANDERING

Then the Lord God called to the man, and said to him, "Where are you?" *(Genesis 3:9)*

From a distance, I heard God calling. "Where are you?" The question grew more and more insistent over time until I tuned in. Until I listened.

For more than five years, I had been living for myself. Doing what felt good, what seemed right to me. I hadn't bothered to check in with God even occasionally. I knew better, though. God had saved me from my sins as a teenager. I had chosen to give my life to him, and my heart had changed. For a while, I kept my commitment, but I received no discipleship in those years. With no one to teach me his ways, I drifted far from fellowship with God.

Until God said enough. Enough of my wandering. Enough of my selfishness. Enough of putting other things before him. God didn't slap me upside the head as I deserved. Instead, he whispered to my heart, pursued me with his love.

When I finally heeded God's voice, going to church seemed to be the next logical step. My husband, Jeff, wanted to go too, so we searched a list of churches near the Air Force base where we were stationed in New Hampshire. We picked one at random, and off we went.

We followed this method week after week. Months later, we found a church to attend. With our meager effort, we took a first step toward God.

Not long after, I discovered I was pregnant. Overjoyed, I called the obstetrician to set up prenatal visits. Pregnancy for me was easy. Except for high blood pressure, I enjoyed good health and had no morning sickness. I continued life as normal, working long hours. Emotions yo-yoed between ecstatic and scared witless at the reality of a baby in my life.

In early fall, I went to the doctor for a checkup. "Next visit, you'll be due for a routine screening," Dr. Marchant said.

"For what?"

The doctor said the alpha-fetal protein test (AFP) detected neural tube defects in unborn babies. "The blood test is a simple, safe procedure. We'll set you up for labs next month if you want it."

"You mean like spina bifida?" I had volunteered with March of Dimes as a teen, but I possessed only a vague awareness of the condition. Dr. Marchant nodded and expounded on the possible abnormalities. The AFP could also indicate the possibility of Down syndrome. If the screening were positive, I would need further tests, including amniocentesis.

"Would knowledge of a problem before birth help you to treat me?" I asked.

"It wouldn't change the way we care for you prior to giving birth," he answered. "It's up to you."

"Can I let you know at the next appointment?"

"That's fine," Dr. Marchant answered, and we wrapped up the appointment.

Jeff worked overnight monitoring security systems on the military flightline, so I came home to an empty house.

As I puttered about in solitude, my thoughts returned to the suggested screening. If Dr. Marchant did not need to be aware of a problem in advance, there was only one other reason to know.

Abortion. If the labs revealed a defect, I would face a major decision.

I didn't want to put such a weighty decision off until later. I'd never choose to have an abortion. I knew firsthand abortion's devastating effect on both baby and mom. I had learned long after the fact my mom had an abortion when I was a child. Her life changed forever. I've often wondered over the years about my unknown sibling.

Right there in the cozy shadows of my tiny kitchen, my heart spoke to God's heart. *If there's something wrong with my baby, God, I'm going to trust you. I'm not having the test.*

My decision was simple and final. Though I had ignored God for years, the prayer leaped into my mind. Once breathed, the choice settled the matter for me. So settled, in fact, I never even confided about my angst to Jeff.

The next few months passed by much as usual—as ordinary as life gets when you're expecting your first baby. Christmas visiting with family came and went. My blood pressure soared, but the doc monitored my health, and I felt no ill effects. My waist size increased until my toes were no longer visible.

Jeff and I threw ourselves into preparations for our baby. Friends and family showered us with everything we needed for our nest. I crocheted a blanket and painted white onesies in patterns suitable for either a boy or girl. After we found the perfect crib, Jeff assembled it in a corner of our loft bedroom. I prewashed the pastel bedding and smoothed out the sheet and comforter. Jeff fastened a mobile with bright animals dancing out of reach of tiny fingers which would one day stretch out in wonder. Arm in arm, we stepped back to admire our handiwork, dreaming of the day we'd hold our already adored firstborn child.

As I look back on this time before Alyssa's birth, I realize God was also preparing. Preparing me, not himself. His eternal eyes see the beginning, middle, and end all at once, so he equipped me with all I'd need to become the mom of a child with Down syndrome. When I was a teen, he had planted the seed of salvation and trust in him. Though faith seemed dead in the ground of my heart, he waited on my readiness to turn to him.

As I wandered from God, he was gracious. In the year before I became pregnant, I felt his tug on my heart, pulling me to his side where I belonged. His pull was a gentle rain softening the seed in my heart and increasing my desire to know him. By the time I stood under the fluorescent lights of Dr. Marchant's office one October afternoon, God had already equipped me to think about my choices with the mind of Christ—I was ready to trust him. His seed's first tender shoots sprouted.

God enabled me to take a baby step of faith alone in our condo. Unlike my normal control-freak self, I experienced complete peace in the months leading up to Alyssa's birth. I never gave another thought to the possibility there could be a problem with our expected baby.

I perceive now Alyssa was the soil conditioner God used to awaken the seed of faith he had long ago buried in my heart.

SOUGHT AND FOUND

We thank you, O God! We give thanks because you are near. People everywhere tell of your wonderful deeds. (Psalm 75:1 NLT)

I lay back on my bed at the birthing center holding Jeff's hand as a nurse bent over her stethoscope pressed deep into the flesh of my swollen belly. As she listened, a frown creased her smooth forehead. "I'm not detecting the baby's heartbeat." A slight edge bit into her calm voice. "Let's turn you over." I complied as quickly as I could, heaving my girth from side to side like a beached whale. "Nope, I'm still not getting it."

The nurse pressed a button and sprang into action. Others swarmed out of the nurse's station to assist. "I'm calling the doctor back in. Your baby needs to come out. Now."

In shock, I rolled onto the gurney hustled into the room by an orderly. My frozen mind couldn't process the questions hovering on the periphery. My eyes sought Jeff.

"Jeff ...?"

His concerned face swam into view above me as the orderly kicked off the brake of the gurney. I felt the bed roll. "He'll be able to follow you soon," an unseen voice answered.

Out in the hallway, the glaring lights overhead and the rush of cool air shocked my senses, releasing a flood of memories from the morning. This was the day. The day we'd meet and hold our baby.

Earlier in the week, my doctor, concerned about high blood pressure and preeclampsia, recommended inducing labor. Though close to the due date, my body showed no sign of spontaneous labor, and he was worried about both my health and the baby's. They scheduled the inducement for Saturday.

We didn't need the buzz of an alarm clock to wake in the morning. The baby bag waited by the door, standing sentinel there for the past six weeks. We arrived at the hospital early, and the staff ushered us into a comfortable, homey birthing room. No fluorescent lights intruded— only the golden glow of a lamp illuminated the space. Jeff lounged in an armchair while I sat on the bed. We knew we were in for a long day, but the prize was worth any wait.

A nurse took my vitals and injected the labor-inducing drug Pitocin to begin the process. Dr. Marchant popped in for a quick check. "It's gonna be a while," he said, informed by decades of experience.

An hour later, before I experienced a single contraction, nurses rushed me into a sterile, stark white operating room. They bustled about, prepping for surgery. A gowned and masked man appeared—the anesthesiologist. "Dr. Marchant left the hospital, so he'll be a couple more minutes," he said. "We normally do general anesthesia for emergencies, but I think I'll have the time for an epidural." Shock numbed my mind again. If he were expecting an answer, none came. "Let's get going," he directed the nurse.

True to his word, the anesthesiologist completed the procedure a moment before Dr. Marchant entered to take his place at my feet. A sterile sheet hanging above my chest blocked my line of sight just as the epidural disconnected my brain from the lower half of my body. Or at least that's what they said would happen when they pushed the numbing drug into the space around my spinal cord.

I heard a thin, scared voice. It was mine. "Where's Jeff?" I craned my neck to no avail. More insistently, "Where's Jeff?"

"He's coming. They're getting him into scrubs." The soft voice did little to soothe my fears.

After what seemed like eternity, my eyes found and locked on Jeff watching from across the room. His dark eyes mirrored my own apprehension.

"You'll feel some tugging and pulling," Dr. Marchant said, but I felt so much more. I cried out in pain.

The epidural had only partially kicked in, but the pain didn't last long. Within a moment, the doctor yanked Alyssa from her secure, warm cocoon into the cold, forbidding world of the operating room.

"You have a girl!"

I glimpsed my newborn baby as Dr. Marchant raised her above the screen barrier like Simba in *The Lion King*. I heard no sound. Even an inexperienced mother such as I knew she should cry. Alarm bells rang in my shocked mind. A nurse, all business, whisked Alyssa out the door, motioning for Jeff to follow.

"She'll be all right. She's in good hands." Dr. Marchant reassured me as he set to work suturing my incision. As he bent to the task, he wisecracked to those remaining in the room, "Let's make sure we get everything out. She knows some good lawyers." He was an old friend and client of the senior partner at the law firm where I worked as an accountant.

By this time, the epidural had fully kicked in. I lay there, staring at the shiny ceiling, teeth chattering. As he finished stitching my long incision, Dr. Marchant piped up. "Oh, we forgot to note the time of birth." He straightened to glance over his shoulder at the clock on the wall and turned to me. "Let's say ... 10:52." He recorded the official time on her birth certificate, though only God knew the real time.

I stared up at ceiling tiles passing by as an orderly wheeled me to another room for recovery. My dazed mind struggled to catch up with the events of the day. Soon Jeff joined me there. "We have a baby girl." He beamed as he sat next to me, pressing his lips to my limp hand.

A few minutes later, a nurse entered, followed by a white coat. "I'm Dr. Martinez." He smiled. "I'm the pediatrician who attended your baby's birth. You've been through quite an ordeal."

The nurse rounded the foot of my bed and stood to my right.

I nodded, wondering where Alyssa was. "Is my baby all right?"

"She's fine." He paused, shifting his gaze from me to Jeff and back again, and took a deep breath. "But she has a condition called Down syndrome." He launched into a description of characteristics which led him to diagnose Alyssa. Wide-set almond-shaped eyes. A single line across the palm of her hands. Low muscle tone. Small hands and feet. White spots in her irises (which lend her bluish-hazel eyes unique beauty). At the same time, I felt a tissue pressed into my right hand. Distracted, I wondered why. The nurse probably thought I would need it to mop up tears after receiving the news. Meanwhile, Dr. Martinez painted a hopeful picture of our future and promised to return with resources for us. I didn't take in half of what he said. A surreal moment, for sure.

The duo left, but the nurse immediately returned with Alyssa. Our baby. Cradling her in my arms for the first time, I stared, amazed. Dark eyelashes rested in slumber upon dusky rounded cheeks. I wondered if the rocky entrance into the outside world tuckered her out. Tiny lips pursed and sucked. My hand lingered on her soft dark brown hair, just enough hair for me to claim she wasn't bald. I longed to unwrap her swaddling to examine all her miniature fingers and toes, but I was afraid I might wake her. My new mother instincts told me not to disturb a sleeping child.

I tore my gaze away to look at Jeff. "Well, what do you think?" I grinned.

"We almost lost her today." His face clouded at the thought. I realized both our perspectives had changed after the trauma of Alyssa's birth. We were simply grateful. Thankful to be holding our baby. Down syndrome was not relevant to our gratitude.

"Let's thank God," I said. We were entering new territory. For the first time, we bowed our heads together, and Jeff prayed over Alyssa. Our talk with God was nothing scripted or spiritual. Just two immature children expressing gratitude to their Father in heaven, committing to trust him with whatever came our way.

COLLISION COURSE

You made all the delicate, inner parts of my body and knit me together in my mother's womb. Thank you for making me so wonderfully complex! Your workmanship is marvelous—how well I know it. (Psalm 139:13–4 NLT)

Down syndrome.

Alyssa's diagnosis crashed into my world one icy March morning, but it sank in over time. Before long, though, I understood, at five pounds, thirteen ounces, this tiny, new human being would rock everything I had known.

I grew up as the fifth of six children. My father was a proud man, especially of his own intellect. He taught his children to esteem intelligence above all else. God blessed me with a quick mind, so I excelled in school. In those formative years, my parents affirmed me for only one thing—being smart. I learned to feel confident and secure in the ability to apply myself to anything and succeed. I would even say I understood from my family my worth depended on my intellect.

In Alyssa's early days and months, I was so busy and stressed I had no time to think about philosophical notions such as human value. I recovered from surgery and returned to work after six weeks of leave. Home life revolved around Alyssa's many needs. Because of low muscle tone, sucking was slow. Feeding times overlapped as I spent hours coaxing milk into her hungry belly. Appointments with doctors and therapists rushed into every gap in the schedule like water fills storm drains during a flood. A mountain of therapeutic instructions we received consumed any extra time. At the end of the year, we moved from New Hampshire to Pennsylvania. Jeff downgraded from Air Force active duty to reserve status, and I started a new job as manager of the accounting department for a private business.

As we settled into some semblance of a routine, I frequently pondered the myriad events of the prior year. The headliner, of course, was Alyssa's diagnosis. At the beginning, I knew almost nothing. My limited experience of the condition came from a kid in my neighborhood named Johnny. I think he was much older than I, but I can't really be sure. He often stood alone in his front yard, waving as our school bus passed.

I devoured anything I could get my hands on to satisfy my craving for more information. Much of the literature offered dismal facts, leading me to believe there was a possibility my child might never walk, run, or talk. The R word—retarded—surfaced as inevitable. My precious baby would never have normal intelligence. Would she even be able to learn?

What, I wondered, was Alyssa's value? I needed to address this pivotal question head on.

If I believed her life had value, and I instinctively did, my understanding of what gave a person significance was flawed. If she had worth superseding what she could do or give, from where did her significance originate?

Hashing all this out over a tiny baby I loved with my whole heart may seem crazy. People rarely rationalize such things. Instead, we often assign value to human life informed by parental treatment and life experiences.

Some believe beauty provides special worth. Others derive value from their parental roles. Still more hold fast to possessions, job titles, or power. All these sooner or later disappoint. They shift and change.

Jesus compared houses built on two different types of ground—rock and sand. He declared the rock to be the wise place to build. Any other foundation for building proves unreliable. Beauty fades, intelligence diminishes, power subsides, and property deteriorates. Even if these attributes held value for a while, I assumed Alyssa would likely never attain them. I combed through the Bible for a more trustworthy foundation for her worth. My concept of her value, along with my own, depended on this quest.

Though my faith was minute at this point in my life, I realized my perception of the value of human beings was upside down and backward from God's view. Man says worth comes from abilities and what we contribute to the world. God says worth comes from the fact he created us and gives purpose. The value he instills in us does not depend on any transitory quality of this life.

My mind pivoted as I grasped the beautiful truth intellect is *not* what makes us valuable. Brainpower is not what makes Alyssa valuable. I released the need to judge worth and became free to accept her (and, yes, even myself and others) the way God made her.

Since then, Alyssa has grown into a beautiful young woman with a unique personality. Her abilities are many and varied. She never met a book she didn't like to read— particularly Shakespeare. Her vocabulary would earn a high SAT score. She enjoys working and volunteering. Yet none of these contributions to the world determine her intrinsic worth.

These days, reflecting on the moment in the hospital recovery room when I first heard the words "Down syndrome" makes me chuckle. The head-on collision of my ideas and reality shocked me. I never saw the crash coming, but God did. He knew I needed my world shaken to cause me to shed beliefs built on a loose, sandy foundation.

So he sent Alyssa.

FIRST THINGS FIRST

But seek first His kingdom and His righteousness, and
all these things will be added to you. (Matthew 6:33)

No single expert or book hands out a scroll with all the
"Thou shalts" and "Thou shalt nots" of Down syndrome.
I shuttled Alyssa to many experts in those early days.
All offered sage advice. Over the course of the first few
months, I filled my notebook with what I learned. Thus, I
created a to-do list which governed my days.

In my first week of recovery from the C-section, I
jumped onto the merry-go-round of Down syndrome and
hung on with all my might. The first appointment was
with the cardiologist. Next up—the geneticist. Then back
to the pediatrician for additional referrals to feeding and
early intervention specialists. Along with a series of follow-
up visits to the first few doctors, she received the services
of a teacher and of occupational, physical, and speech
therapists. Some specialists provided in-home services.
Others were scattered far and wide. The schedule exhausted
me. At each therapy appointment, I received homework for
activities to help Alyssa grow and develop. The list grew.

My dear hubby and I also sought out and attended a
support group. As newbies to this world, we could offer
nothing, but the experienced parents shared their knowledge

about advocacy, rights, and responsibilities. We soaked up everything we heard, and I added more to the list.

Insurance issues bombarded us. Within a few months, benefit statements and bills stuffed our mailbox. We had two health insurance companies involved, both of which tried to foist primary responsibility on the other. Neither processed claims efficiently. Every day I spent hours—yes hours, in the middle of my full-time job—on the phone attempting to unwind the tangle of statements and payouts. The confused paperwork stretched my professional accounting skills. I added another section to the list.

Every parent has a profound desire to do their best for their children. I'm no exception. I worked so hard to figure out what was needed and how to get it, but my motivation ran much deeper. As time passed, I realized my determination also stemmed from worry about the unknown future. Though an imagined future is never guaranteed, parents of typical kids make a lot of assumptions, most of which come true. I didn't have the luxury of that mindset. Also, though I never spoke the words, I harbored a deep sense Alyssa's chance of success all depended on me. I thought what I did could make or break her future.

The disability community showed me how to help Alyssa reach her full potential. By the world's standard, she needed to become a productive citizen. Productivity involved achievements like crawling, talking, walking, reading, writing, working, and, ultimately, living independently. Nothing on this list in and of itself is a wrong aspiration.

But I discovered I had the wrong priorities.

There's an old philosophical illustration floating around about packing rocks into a jar. As the story goes, a professor has a jar with sand, pebbles, and rocks. He first adds the sand, then the pebbles. When he tries to put the rocks in, the jar is already too full, and they won't fit. Then the teacher produces another empty jar. This time he places the rocks into the jar first. Next, he adds the pebbles, and finally the sand. *Voilà.* Everything fits.

I needed to learn what were rocks, pebbles, and sand on my list.

After a grueling first year with Alyssa, God led our family to a church and introduced us to his ways. One Sunday morning, the pastor taught from verses in Matthew. He said we should be like the flowers and birds who do not worry about the future. Those carefree flowers and birds cast a shadow of doubt over my list.

The pastor moved on to the final verse of the chapter. Verse thirty-three is a clear statement of God's priorities. His kingdom. His righteousness. Now the light glared, highlighting the error of my list. *Okay, God, I got the message.* Over the next few days, I meditated on these words and asked God to show me his best for Alyssa's life.

No one told me I had permission to say no to the list. Now God showed me a new order of importance. First, though, I had to admit, with chagrin, God's priority did not even appear on my list. Like the professor in the adage who filled a new jar, I wrote a new list. First thing— seek God's kingdom and his righteousness. Jeff and I understood we should strive first and foremost to teach Alyssa to know, love, and serve God.

Some may wonder about this priority for a person with Down syndrome or another intellectual disability. Some may question if a person with a lower IQ possesses the capability to know, love, and serve God. An emphatic yes is the simple answer to the question. God created each one, including Alyssa, for fellowship with him. Would a flawless God somehow mess up and make a person who couldn't receive him?

Soon after Alyssa's first birthday, Jeff and I dedicated her to the Lord. In the service, we claimed Matthew 6:33 as the guiding verse for her life. From then on, we asked God to help us to keep his perspective, always pointing her to him.

Of course, I still hoped for a good outcome for the other items on my list, but I relaxed on life's merry-go-round. I got off the sleek horse scrolling up and down in time to the organ music. Instead, I sat and relaxed on the sleigh. Underlying worry and fear dissipated as I recognized God, and not I, is in control of the one he created. I didn't change immediately, but over time I learned to be content with whatever life skills or academic success God chose to give Alyssa.

God's priorities trump mine every time.

DREAM BIG

Where there is no vision, the people are unrestrained.
(Proverbs 29:18)

"What is your vision for Alyssa?"

I first heard this concept at a national Down syndrome conference when she was two years old. I almost laughed out loud. Inside, I blew it off. *What an absurd question.*

At the time, Alyssa, a tiny pre-toddler, did not yet walk or talk. Even under normal circumstances, how does a new parent describe what their child will become in a few years, let alone twenty? I left the workshop shaking my head. Yet, over the next few days, the idea swirled in my mind like gauzy cotton candy around a paper tube. Designing a vision statement for her became my new challenge.

As an accounting manager, I knew quite well the concept within the corporate context. Business Dictionary defines a vision statement as "an aspirational description of what an organization would like to achieve or accomplish in the mid-term or long-term future." Far more than a murky pipe dream, business vision encompasses attainable, quantifiable, and ideological goals for the future. I had never thought about applying these same ideas to a life plan.

Furthermore, vision defines a clear purpose. Business Dictionary continues: "It is intended to serve as a clear guide for choosing current and future courses of action." Though not all goals are attained, no one creates goals they don't intend to achieve. Organizations use the statement as a plumb line to stay on course toward a planned outcome.

Because my analytical mind gravitates toward cause and effect in planning, I applied my business knowledge to Alyssa's future. I struggled, though, with the leap from business to personal. In the corporate world, you set measurable goals—sell so many widgets at such and such a profit margin to exceed a stated bottom line. How in the world do you apply the concept to a person's life? In business, we understand some of the possibilities, but I had no idea what might happen with Alyssa. I had barely even met another person with Down syndrome. Sparse public information, most of which was negative, limited my understanding of her potential. Additionally, individuals in the Down syndrome community possess such a wide range of abilities. How could I fathom what to dream for her?

The book of Proverbs warns those who lack vision. The concept in this context differs from mere aspirations or goals. Proverbs refers to revelation from God, an understanding of his ways. Without insight from God, we have no plan, no map to follow. Life's journey becomes following a series of whims with no clear direction. We are prone to wander and never reach our intended destination.

I started dreaming for Alyssa by fusing the business and spiritual concepts of vision. I yearned for God's revelation. After all, hadn't he created her? Didn't he already know the days he ordained for her "... when as yet there was not one of them."? (Psalm 139:16). Through prayer, waiting, and listening, his wisdom became my source.

With enthusiasm and God's inspiration, I dug into the details, breaking down life into its parts—relationships, spirituality, education, employment, home life, service. After subdividing each of those sections into goals, I wrote specific statements about the opportunities I coveted for Alyssa in twenty years. Instinctively, I listed typical life goals and modified as I perceived a need.

Opportunity. This word wouldn't leave me. I couldn't predict her future. But my vision turned into a manifesto of the opportunities I believed and hoped would be available to her as an adult.

My business experience taught me the vision should steer choices we made for Alyssa. The verse in Proverbs supported my understanding. Without this guide rail, we often select options based on momentary feelings and strengths or weaknesses. Emotions, though, almost always aim at nothing, or worse, the wrong thing. They usually lead us astray. I needed to transcend the current day and point toward the future by asking the question, "Will this action help or hinder her to achieve a target opportunity as an adult?"

How did this flesh-out on a day-to-day, year-to-year basis? In the realm of education, we sought an inclusive setting with minimal modifications to curriculum so Alyssa might graduate from high school. We encouraged friendships with a variety of children to pave the way toward future acceptance in work and social settings. We chose therapists who focused not only on needs but also on strengths, so she would learn to capitalize on her assets. In all these cases and many others, we knew if we did not develop these attitudes and opportunities in childhood, they would not materialize in adulthood.

As difficult as the process of writing a vision statement was, the reality of working toward the goals proved far more complex and arduous. I had no clue about all the challenges in those early days. I skipped along the sunny road toward opportunity, oblivious of the boulders and potholes looming ahead threatening to create detours in the journey.

Our all-seeing God was, and still is, controlling the direction of Alyssa's life. Some of the opportunities we dreamed about became reality. Others did not. I am not disappointed. Like the psalmist, I know "the nearness of God is [her] good" (Psalm 73:28).

THE POWER OF A SONG

A person has joy in an apt answer, and how delightful
is a timely word! (Proverbs 15:23)

Tightly wound. Those words describe my mental state
during Alyssa's early years. Some days, I barely held
myself together. Other days, I fell apart.

Within a twenty-four-month window of time, we had
checked off several items on the list of top ten most
stressful life events. A new baby. Immediate medical
complications. A move to a new state to be closer to family.
A new job. I also needed to locate doctors and service
providers for Alyssa, make new social connections, and
unravel a bureaucratic snarl of insurance problems. Did I
mention selling our old home in a depressed market and
finding a new one? To top off the stress, Alyssa required
surgeries to correct problems with her eye muscles.

The whirlwind afforded no time to attend to the
emotions accompanying these changes. For better or for
worse, those were sacrificed on the altar of productivity.
Controlled by the tyranny of the urgent, I shoved my
feelings to the back burner for years.

But even the back burner has heat. After a long, slow
simmer, my emotions boiled over.

The catalyst was a song. To be more precise, the lyrics
of a song. The thirty-minute drive to work each morning

gave me time to relax. To listen to music and sing my heart out as I whizzed down the highway. I bebopped along one morning when a song, "Sometimes Miracles Hide," by Bruce Carroll, came on the radio. This soulful ballad recounts the journey of a couple who are having a baby. Before birth, the baby is diagnosed with a problem. Several poignant verses describe some of the events in the first few years of the child's life. The song concludes with a reminder God's blessings appear in surprising ways and often take time to be realized.

The floodgates of my heart opened. Emotions poured through all the steely barriers I had erected. I fought to maintain enough control to drive the car as sobs racked my body. It was an ugly, messy cry. Thanks to waterproof makeup, I didn't arrive at work with raccoon eyes. I grimaced at my puffy, red face in the rearview mirror before I slid out of the vehicle and ducked into the building. Once in the sanctuary of my office, I pulled myself together. Duty called.

As I threw myself into work, my surging emotions receded back into their compartment. I spent my day analyzing balance sheets, evaluating sales reports, reviewing overdue accounts receivable, settling employee complaints, and managing a tax audit. With plenty of immediate tasks to capture my attention, I didn't think much more about my earlier catharsis.

Alyssa's bedtime routine always kept us busy, so Jeff and I didn't have a chance to catch up until later in the evening.

"Have you ever heard the song 'Sometimes Miracles Hide'?" I asked as we plopped onto the couch. He hadn't. Jeff is more of a country music fan. Since this was before the time of the internet and Google, I couldn't immediately access the tune for him. I did my best to explain the meaning and its impact on me.

"Sounds nice," he said. I decided I should buy the CD so he could listen for himself.

Meanwhile, I kept hearing the song on the radio. When the CD arrived in the mail, I listened over and over, morning after morning, during what became a regular window of blessed emotional release (aka losing it).

Before I heard the song, I understood its message—at least in my head. I knew Alyssa was a gift from God created according to his exact specifications. I knew he made no mistakes. I knew she blessed me. I knew God had a purpose. I knew God would see us through the struggles. I knew and believed these truths, but the song's message touched deeper than knowledge.

Until I heard those lyrics for the first time, I didn't realize I was barely clinging to hope. The slender thread of my faith stretched taut. I exerted an extraordinary amount of determination and tenacity to hold beliefs which were, at the time, mostly unfulfilled. I've since learned this is the very essence of faith. "Now faith is the certainty of things hoped for, a proof of things not seen" (Hebrews 11:1). By acknowledging my struggle, this song affirmed and strengthened my trust in God.

The fourth verse of the ballad picks up the family's story with the daughter going to school by bus—an ordinary, everyday, taken-for-granted activity for children. Though their child has differences, the parents rejoice through tears she is growing and thriving. This simple story whispered into my own future all would be well, whatever the circumstance. I would bear no regrets walking the journey designated for me by God.

The song also awakened my emotional senses to an acute loneliness I harbored. Though Jeff and I had met a few other parents on the same path of life, conversation centered on pragmatics. How to feed. Types of therapy.

Medical issues. We had not dug into the nitty-gritty, messy, jumbled emotions which go along with having a child who has differences. Truth be told, I probably had not been ready for a deep dive into the muddle. Now this song revealed my underlying need. The words offered sweet reassurance others sit in the boat with me. They too have navigated the same murky waters, wondering if God can be trusted.

I had imagined I could avoid the complicated emotions and the even more difficult inevitable questions they prompted about God. My relationship with God would not go deeper until tested. I believe God chose a simple song to expose the fears, doubts, questions, and hurts I had plated over with self-protective armor. Then, with love and compassion, he proved himself faithful by satisfying my deepest needs.

No one wants to lose it. Losing sounds—and often feels—distressing. But I believe God brought an apt answer, as the proverb says, through the words of a simple song. His answer was for me to lose control. To lose my iron grip on all the feelings I suppressed. In so doing, I gained God's presence and peace.

WRONG FOCUS

Man looks at the outward appearance, but the LORD
looks on the heart. (1 Samuel 16:7)

Excitement mingled with apprehension as we
contemplated preschool for Alyssa the fall after she turned
three years old. She had now begun to walk without much
help, and our church offered an excellent classroom
environment. We had orchestrated a plan with the school
much earlier in the year, and our hopes soared.

Though we had prior experience in a school system,
worry crept into our excitement. Alyssa had received various
types of intervention services since she was two weeks
old. Most recently, she'd attended a preschool program
through the public-school early intervention system with
other toddlers identified with developmental delays. Now
she would enter preschool in our neighborhood with her
typical peers for the first time.

As usual in the disability world, we met *ad nauseum*
to prepare for the school year. My first discussion with
the preschool director yielded a willingness to try this
crazy new (to them) idea of inclusion. I knew no mandate
required them to make accommodations for Alyssa, so I
felt grateful for their commitment to make a place for her.
Then came the real work of building a plan.

Over the next few months, I met with teachers and support service personnel to develop the preschool equivalent of an individualized education plan. Identifying strengths and needs provided a platform for creating goals. We also examined the classroom environment and curriculum for any necessary modifications and supports. Last, we brainstormed strategies for achieving success. All in all, this productive beginning encouraged me.

I held Alyssa's hand as we negotiated the steps down to the basement level entrance on the first day of preschool. We went inside the brick building, but I hesitated at the door of the classroom. Jitters ping-ponged in my mind. I'm sure I had more nerves than Alyssa on the warm fall day.

"You ready?" I tossed a bright smile I didn't quite feel down to my tiny toddler. She marched in and greeted her teacher, Miss Suzy. I surveyed the room. Friendly painted tigers peeped out from behind vivid leafy fronds to smile at colorful parrots on the cement wall's mural. A bulletin board adorned with sun, clouds, rain, and snow awaited eager young learners' attention. A poster illustrated in pictures declared the desired manners for the fifteen wide-eyed boys and girls. A sensory table invited exploring hands to touch and feel. A blue nylon pocket calendar stood ready to mark the days and promise of the coming year.

"Welcome, Alyssa." With a smile, Miss Suzy ushered her to one of the round tables set on colorful area rugs. A Polaroid camera whirred and produced her picture to pin to a board on the wall. Without further ado, my baby began school.

Alyssa thrived at preschool. Miss Suzy and the administrators went the extra mile to create success. She participated in all activities with the other children. Together they counted, identified letters, sang songs, and learned nursery rhymes. Time outdoors provided an important part of learning where she developed both physically and socially. There, the developmental goal of interactive play emerged. She felt a deep sense of belonging in her preschool environment.

Of course, nothing comes without troubles. Alyssa most often used sign language because of delayed speech, so the other kids could not always understand her communication. As an impulsive wanderer, she sometimes left her carpet square during circle time to investigate whatever caught her eye. She often did not appear to be paying attention to the teacher. We had a good system for addressing concerns though. When they surfaced, the teacher and I would talk either in person or on the phone to find solutions to reinforce both at home and at school.

Stairs. One surprising issue arose and persisted throughout the year. Yes, walking up and down the stairs to and from the classroom created great consternation for the teachers. Because of her gross motor delays, low muscle tone, and diminutive stature, Alyssa had a tough time on stairs. Though carrying her would have been easier and faster, we insisted she walk because she needed the practice to grow stronger. Unfortunately, her slow pace disrupted the timing and flow of the entire classroom.

This limitation had no immediate, viable solution. Alyssa required time to develop her motor skills. We persevered with her ongoing physical therapy, tried to focus on the positives, and went on with life at preschool.

Near the end of the school year, Miss Suzy invited parents into the classroom for a celebration. She opened with a reenactment of circle time. All the children sat cross-legged on the floor, eyes glued on their teacher. All except Alyssa. Her eyes roamed the room full of strange, fawning faces. She wiggled and got up, but an assistant helped her find her place again. Next, the kids sang songs and recited nursery rhymes they had learned. Alyssa found her time to shine. She belted out every word and motion.

I could hear the surprised whispers around me. "Look at how well she knows the songs."

In the final part of the program, Miss Suzy presented an award to each child in alphabetical order by last name. A novice at preschool norms, I had not expected this nice affirmation. Miss Suzy went down the alphabet, giving a fancy certificate to each child. Artistic. Good manners. Cheerful. Helpful. Friendly. So she continued until Alyssa, last in line, was called.

The award was ... wait for it ... Best Stair Stepper.

Everyone clapped. I clapped and beamed. Alyssa was so proud as she, true to her dramatic nature, swept into a deep curtsy before the audience. We all laughed and applauded again.

Well satisfied with the year's progress, we thanked Miss Suzy and the school's director and went home.

Later, though, my thoughts kept returning to the awards. Something about Alyssa's rankled. As I turned the moniker over and over in my mind, I realized her award was the only one that did not denote character or true achievement. The awards given to the other children described a strength they either latently possessed or developed over the course of the year. Her award highlighted a weakness. She had not even progressed much in walking throughout her time at preschool. In fact, mobility on stairs remains a challenge to this day.

This slight wasn't such a big deal I took offense or held a grudge. Nor did I see the need to address my concern with the teacher or administration of the school. I felt sad the physical limitation drew such focus and overshadowed the more important inner characteristics we should celebrate.

I realize I too share such tendencies. I sometimes highlight the most obvious and immediate characteristic in another person. Thanks to Alyssa's influence and God's grace, though, I know I must look deeper to see true qualities in the same way God sees the heart.

RISK

Now all these things are from God, who reconciled us to Himself through Christ and gave us the ministry of reconciliation. (2 Corinthians 5:18)

Forgiveness.

Reconciliation.

Simple words to say. Harder to understand. Seemingly impossible to do when you're the one who's devastated.

The pain came from an unexpected place. As a young Christian, I admired most other believers. They seemed to have the Christian life in order. Their relationships appeared perfect. They were all so much more mature than me. Always doing the right thing. Or so I thought.

Alyssa completed her first full year of preschool. Every report we had received throughout the year indicated we had achieved successful inclusion. We had seen such growth, and we loved the staff and other students. Since the preschool was part of our church, we loved these folks as family. She enjoyed seeing her school friends on Sundays too. Though the summer break approached, we already anticipated the next school year.

On the last Friday of preschool, the director invited Jeff and me into her office. The brief, cordial meeting ended with an explosive announcement. "I think it would be best if Alyssa did not come back here next year," she said. "There might be a better placement for her."

I'm not even sure what I replied. I have no idea what Jeff said. All I remember is bolting out of there as fast as possible. I probably muttered something appropriate and polite as I escaped to my car with tears streaming down my face. There, Jeff and I faced one another in stunned confusion and drove home. We had no words to express how blindsided we felt.

I stewed in a mess of sobbing, resentment, and pain all weekend. I couldn't even attend church on Sunday. What, I wondered, could Alyssa have done to warrant kicking her out of preschool? If there were problems, why hadn't they discussed them with me sometime during the preceding year? How could followers of God cast her aside because of her differences? Didn't Jesus command us to love and help "the least of these"? I had learned in the last four years the world doesn't always value her, but I never imagined God's people, my brothers and sisters, would reject my daughter.

Heart shattered, I reverted to old habits. My own childhood experiences were fraught with abandonment and fear. I learned to protect myself at all costs, developing a hard shell to buffer my emotional trauma. I resolved never, ever, to need anyone. If a person rejected me, I wrote them off and moved on without them. I was inclined to do the same with these so-called friends and sisters in Christ.

I had also been studying the Bible and learned about how God tells us to handle offenses within the body of Christ. In Matthew, Jesus said, "If your brother sins, go and show him his fault in private; if he listens to you, you have won your brother" (18:15). The directions for this situation left no wiggle room.

Here's where the business of forgiveness and reconciliation gets tough. I didn't want to do the humbling work. Why should I beg those hypocrites to accept my daughter? My way, leaving them in the dust, seemed better. More satisfying, somehow. I relished the idea of walking away with my head held high, pride intact.

Despite my obstinance, God performed a work of grace in my heart over the weekend. The truth of his word sank in and loosened my grip on stubborn self-will. By Sunday evening, I knew what I must do.

On Monday morning, I broke a chink in my shell and risked further heartache. Shaky fingers punched the phone buttons to the director's office. Voice quivering, I described how hurtful her comments had been. I asked her all the questions plaguing me over the weekend. I didn't accuse, but I explained my point of view.

Her swift, unequivocal answer surprised me almost as much as the original offense. "This has been on my heart all weekend," she said. "And I was wrong."

Her reversal caught me at a loss for words. "Thank you," I finally answered.

She invited Alyssa to enroll in preschool for the next fall. The conclusion was surprisingly simple. God's Spirit had also been prompting her throughout the weekend. He had prepared her for my Monday morning call.

Now I faced a choice. How would I respond? Could I forgive? Forgiveness meant I would stop feeling angry or resentful for the rejection. How could I achieve peace after I'd been cut to the quick? What if she hurt me again?

Should I once again trust the school with my child? Reconciliation takes forgiveness a step further to reestablish relationship. I doubted the prerequisite trust was even possible for me. The director had wounded me at my greatest point of vulnerability—my child.

I decided to punt the decision to another day. "I really appreciate what you said. I'll talk to my husband, and we'll let you know what we will do." I ended the conversation, marveling at the turn of events. The director had no clue the pain she caused with her comments until the Holy Spirit convicted her. At the same time, he equipped me to offer his grace and forgiveness.

In the end, Jeff and I agreed to send Alyssa back to our church preschool. Yes, returning risked my heart as well as Alyssa's well-being, but we had already seen God's hand in this situation. We chose to trust him with our daughter. As a result, she developed and thrived.

The bigger leap in maturity, though, occurred in me. I experienced firsthand the power of God to overcome past and present wounds. He broke a stranglehold of suffering. He proved I don't need to maintain my own shell of protection. When I broke through my own armor to reach out, I found he became my constant shield of defense. I can trust him even in situations with potentially untrustworthy people.

This experience with Alyssa also opened my eyes to an awareness of a role for me in God's kingdom. I experienced my first conscious understanding of God using me to extend his grace and mercy to another person. What a privilege to be the conduit of his character! It all flowed from taking the risk to forgive.

EXPECTATIONS

"I am the Lord, the God of all the peoples of the world.
Is anything too hard for me?" (Jeremiah 32:27 NLT)

Early in the fall, my knees hit the wooden floor in my kitchen at the words I heard on the voicemail. "I'm heading to the medical center with Alyssa." Jeff paused, voice unsteady. "The doctor thinks she may have a brain tumor. They want to run some tests."

After the moment of paralysis, I scrambled into action. I scooped up my purse and keys lying next to me on the floor and bolted for the door. Its slam echoed behind me as I headed for the car. Adrenaline coursed through my body, jangling nerves and tangling thoughts.

As I navigated the brief, yet interminable, drive to the hospital, images and events from the morning flashed through my mind. Alyssa waking before dawn. Crying. Vomiting. Stumbling. Falling. Pitiful attempts to stand again. Confusion clouding her trusting eyes. Alarmed by this, I had contacted the on-call pediatrician. "The vertigo is probably from an inner ear infection," he said. "But bring her in to the office as soon as we open, and we'll take a look."

Jeff had agreed to take her to the doctor's office. I assumed the doc would prescribe an antibiotic to clear up this common infection, so I headed to work. At the office, though, worry nagged at me. Soon after arriving, I called and told Jeff I would come back home soon.

Meanwhile, Jeff took Alyssa to the doctor, who sent him straight to the hospital. Before going there, he called home and left the frightening message which dropped me to the floor.

Ten minutes after racing from my house, I surged through the doors of the emergency department, frantic to learn my four-year old's whereabouts. After I received directions from the receptionist, my high heels clicked a worried path to the radiology department.

"Jeff...?" I opened the door to a dimly lit, private waiting room furnished with children's décor and toys.

Jeff stood, shoulders hunched, his back to the door. He turned. "They have her." His voice broke. "Doing a CT scan now."

I collapsed into his arms.

Jeff spoke in a wobbly voice I had never heard before. "Let's pray." Together, we begged God to spare our child.

A while later, a nurse returned Alyssa to us, and we waited for results. Huddled together, we cradled her as if we could protect her from whatever ravaged her lethargic body. We didn't speak the what ifs. Voicing them might confer power. Inwardly, though, I poured out my worries to God.

A knock intruded, and a doctor dressed in a starched lab coat entered. He made introductions, and delivered his verdict. "The scan shows a spot we're concerned about, but we need more information to know what we're seeing. We'd like to do an MRI."

I didn't know much about MRIs, but I'd do anything to help my sick child. "Of course, anything you need." The doctor left, closing the door on the hush of anxiety left in his wake. Soon a nurse bustled in.

"It's going to be a bit of a wait," she said. "They're really backed up in radiology. We'll come get you when the MRI becomes available."

Minutes ... hours ... ticked by. Unaware, we sat on a sofa, taking turns holding Alyssa, neither saying much except occasional senseless small talk. The toys scattered about the cozy room held no interest for her.

My mom arrived, harried and seeking answers. Surprised, I realized the day had waned into evening. The windowless room had disguised the passage of time. Mom produced bags of fast food as we told her what we knew. We ate, not from hunger but because eating lent normalcy to our upside-down world. Alyssa wanted nothing.

More hours passed.

Finally, a soft knock, and a nurse entered with a smile. "It's time. One of you can go in with her if you like."

I'd never come close to an MRI machine before, but my hand shot up like an eager schoolgirl. "I'll go." The nurse explained the procedure and asked questions about our history with metals. I dashed my signature on the required release and thrust my jewelry at Jeff for safekeeping. I stiffened my spine and moved toward the door.

The nurse motioned for me to sit down. "I'll be back in a minute with something to make her sleep."

True to her word, the nurse returned with a small cup. We coaxed orange liquid into Alyssa, and under its spell, she broke into goofy smiles and gazed with new fascination at her waving hands. Finally, she drifted into sleep.

I trailed the nurse to the MRI room with Alyssa's limp form nestled in my arms. There I surrendered my precious cargo to the yawning tunnel. A technician adjusted the tray, engulfing her tiny body in the giant, sterile machine. I settled on the cold tile floor across the dim room, and the technician hustled to the controls.

Clang. Knock, knock, bang. The monster in the room collected images of Alyssa's brain, for how long I do not know. When the scan ended, I rescued her sleeping form from its clutches.

Back in our hospital haven, we settled in for more waiting. Though now quite late, only Alyssa slept. Close to midnight, a doctor appeared.

We leaped up. The moment of reckoning arrived. We steeled ourselves to face the worst. With a wave, the doctor motioned for us to return to our seats. "The MRI is all clear." He smiled. "I don't know how," he said, "but the spot we saw is gone."

Stunned, I gaped like a fish out of water. I had tried to prepare for anything, but I was not prepared for this. I recovered, choking out an answer. "That's ... good ... but ... what's wrong with her?"

Cerebellar ataxia. At the close of the endless day, the doctor rendered his diagnosis, explaining how a virus causes inflammation in the brain. Symptoms should remit with no treatment after a few weeks or months. He advised us to follow up with our pediatrician.

We gathered our things to leave.

As we walked the silent labyrinth of halls to the hospital's exit, emotions trickled, then flowed over the dam of worry inside me. Relief. Gratitude. Joy. A deep shaky breath revived my numbed heart. Jeff, my mom, and I all broke into laughter, the sound bouncing off the walls in the midnight hush. We didn't care.

In the stillness of my car on the way home, a thought occurred. Why was I so shocked by this miracle? I had prayed, yet my expectation remained low. Now my faith swelled with anticipation.

The next day, Alyssa woke up healthy and happy, as if nothing had ever happened. Indeed, she remembers nothing from our awful day. As for me, the days grew even more precious considering the precarious nature of life.

I REMEMBER

Remember that you were once slaves in Egypt, but the Lord your God brought you out with his strong hand and powerful arm. That is why the Lord your God has commanded you to rest on the Sabbath day. (Deuteronomy 5:15 NLT)

A few months later, I had one of those days where nothing went right. My mom and I went to a giant warehouse store with Alyssa, hustling through a massive shopping list. Lines stretched long. Exhausted, we crawled to the checkout and completed our business. Outside, drizzly weather greeted us. I ran ahead to the car to open the door and strap Alyssa into her safety seat while Mom trailed behind me with the overflowing cart.

Once I occupied Alyssa with a book, I dashed around back to help load the van. Mom already opened the hatch. We shoveled the groceries into our boxes and bags as rain dripped down our necks. After she removed the last item from the cart, Mom did something uncharacteristic. Instead of walking the cart to the return, she shoved it. The cart area was located right next to my vehicle. It shouldn't have been a problem.

Unfortunately, the massive cart strayed from its intended path. *Scrape*. My rear quarter panel lost the contest of cart versus van. Then Mom did something even more uncharacteristic. "S&%t!" The naughty word flew out of her mouth in sheer frustration.

Alyssa, who had never heard such a word in her four years on the earth, parroted her beloved Mamoo. And she repeated it. Over and over. The word tasted quite delicious to her tongue. Her enunciation would have made her speech therapist proud.

Poor Mom. The one who never, ever cussed happened to slip up and taught her young granddaughter her first swear word. Mom was mortified. After Mom's blunder, I realized Alyssa was always listening. Even when she didn't appear to be paying attention, she always remembered.

I've seen this happen time and again throughout the years. Teachers often reported Alyssa played with papers in class, but they were later surprised when she knew the material. When she participated in a singing group, she watched the other kids during rehearsals, but at home she repeated all the words and motions for the songs. At theater practice, she learned every actor's lines so well she prompted others when their memories failed.

These days, in a room full of people, Alyssa, while absorbed in a book, can reply to numerous conversations. Even from another room, she hears and will remind me of comments I've made in passing.

Alyssa's memory would rival the proverbial elephant. She astounds people with her recall of dialogue from movies after only one viewing. She knows the Bible so well she skunks everyone in Bible trivia games. She's my go-to when I want to remember a task. All I need to do is ask her to remind me. Sooner or later, she will inevitably say, "Mom, you need to …" She keeps track of shopping lists, errands, library books, and much more. I love having my own human Alexa device. Her uncanny ability also keeps me accountable to fulfill my promises. If I don't, she'll nag me.

Great recall is a wonderful asset. Sometimes, however, memories trap pain and anxiety in Alyssa's mind and heart. A sad or scary news report from a faraway place overheard during a brief wait in the doctor's office feels personal. A traumatic event from years ago seems like yesterday.

In third grade, her school implemented a fluoride program of which I was unaware until years later. To this day, she shudders at the thought of "swish," as they called the pink fluoride, because it tasted so abhorrent to her. This is one minor example among many.

Unfortunately, Alyssa has endured heartache and bears much heavier burdens.

Is a good memory a Down syndrome thing? Maybe. Probably because of Alyssa's intellectual disability, time is not always linear in her brain. Most of our minds store memories in file cabinets of the past for later recall when necessary. I can't say for sure, but I don't think her mind works this way. She often refers to events from long ago as if they happened yesterday and sometimes, even in the present moment. A listener must cross-examine her to ascertain where the incident falls on a timeline. Because of this quirk in her brain, both old and new memories seem acute and current.

I've often reflected on God's purpose for memory. He creates minds with the ability to recall the past, giving many instructions to his people concerning remembrance. We should memorize his words. We remind ourselves of his character and love for us. He tells us to remember the weak and poor of the world. We should celebrate God's wonderful deeds from the past. Because we're prone to ingratitude, the Bible warns us not to forget God's benefits, and even God himself.

Our memories cannot compare to God's ability to remember. He never forgets us. Our joys. Our worries. Our affliction, shame, and pain. He always cares.

Some days, I celebrate Alyssa's crazy good memory. At other times, when past troubles loom large, I wish I could erase them like I swipe away dry erase marker from my white board. To balance my ambivalence, I help her notice and remember God's presence within those difficult experiences. What was he doing? How did he carry her through?

As a mom, I wrestled with the blessing and curse of Alyssa's exceptional gift of recall. Out of the internal disorder, one thing became clear—God's love endures forever. The umbrella of God's ever-present tender love provides shelter and rest for her heart from the torrent of ever-present memories.

"God's love endures forever," I remind Alyssa every night as I nestle the covers close about her.

She smiles and leans up for a hug and kiss. "I remember, Mom. God's love endures forever."

CHRISTMAS IN SLOW MOTION

In everything give thanks; for this is God's will for you
in Christ Jesus. (1 Thessalonians 5:18)

Slow. Steady. Deliberate.

We do not usually associate these adjectives with children
on Christmas morning. I remember as a kid creeping at the
crack of winter's dawn to sit with bated breath at the top of
the stairs. My siblings and I passed the time by whispering
speculations about what might be hidden under the tree.
Eventually, the gatekeeper, aka Mother, terminated the
excruciating wait. Without a second's hesitation, a herd of
six human elephants stampeded, bumping and thumping
down the wooden stairs in record time. A brief but intense
flurry of flying wrapping paper and bows punctuated by
happy shouts followed.

In my young adult years before Alyssa, we often
celebrated Christmas morning with extended family. The
routine mirrored my childhood experience. Surrounded by
nieces and nephews, my heart delighted in the traditional
yuletide hubbub.

When Alyssa came onto the scene and grew up enough
to be interested in Christmas activities, she opened a
whole new world to me, a holiday in which time and speed
decelerated—where cost and size made no difference. She

opened gifts in the same way one would taste and savor rich chocolate mousse.

When she was a toddler, she didn't know how to open packages. Jeff and I demonstrated unwrapping, often helping her manage the tape and colorful paper. She did not have the inclination to tear through one present after another. After unwrapping each one, she paused to examine and play with it. Her sedate process could last for hours. With only the three of us for Christmas, we delighted in our baby girl so much we never questioned the slow process.

The next year, we spent the holiday with my brother's family. He had three children who were a few years ahead of Alyssa. Christmas dawned, and my brother's kids were up bright and early, waiting for their parents, poised to pounce upon the mountain of Christmas glory surrounding the glittering tree. Alyssa was not a morning person—not even on Christmas. I prodded her to get moving so she wouldn't miss out on the fun.

We finally joined the eager throng in the living room. I nestled Alyssa among the packages strewn on the floor around the tinseled Douglas fir. My sister-in-law, playing Santa, doled out surprises to each child. They ripped through the thin barrier between them and the mystery beneath. Their excitement mingled with the shiny green and red balls of crumpled paper scattered about us. As quickly as they opened each gift, they cast it aside and another took its place.

Mesmerized, Alyssa watched the boisterous scene, mouth agape. At our encouragement, though, she unwrapped her first box. Prying up a corner of paper with her immature pincer grasp, she pulled back a thin strip. She tore the wrap, bit by bit, until we could identify what it contained. Next to her lay a pile of paper useful for making a papier-mâché project. She gasped with joy at the book she'd received and settled in to read, captivated by the illustrations. Interest in any other present vanished.

By now, a stack of loot piled up by each niece and nephew. They were already unwrapping their fifth or sixth gift. Meanwhile, Alyssa's unopened stack begged for attention, but she wasn't ready to move on from her new book. We coaxed her to work her way through all the presents, but not without a thorough investigation of each one before turning to the next. We celebrated Christmas in slow motion.

The same scenario replayed at birthday parties. We never reminded Alyssa to read the cards first. Once she could read, she read aloud, enunciating every word, delighting in the pictures and well-wishes. Sometimes the wrapping itself became a source of amusement and distraction from the main event. Crinkly tissue paper fascinated her. Sooner or later, she opened the bright package. Again, she was content with the first one. Of course, the children attending the party hopped about in excitement as they anticipated watching her open what they brought. "Open mine, open mine!" they said as she plodded through all the birthday bounty.

Despite the lengthy process, I never doubted Alyssa enjoyed her gifts. She appreciated a coloring book as much as an electronic gadget. Since she had learned to sign early in life, she touched palm to mouth to gesture her thanks. Her obvious pleasure and interest in each one gave joy to the givers, and she never compared hers to what others received.

As an adult, Alyssa's outlook on birthdays and Christmas has shifted to a more typical attitude. In the past, she never made a wish list. If someone asked, she would say she desired books or movies. Now she says, "I hope I get lots of presents." She thinks in advance about what she hopes to receive. Now she cares more about quantity, and she rips through the pretty wrapping paper in record time. I guess all those years of occupational therapy finally paid off. Even with these changes, she still finds happiness and satisfaction with simple things—coloring books, fine-point markers, DVDs, and clothing, though her favorites are tickets to movies, concerts, and theater shows.

Some ask, "Is her contentment a Down syndrome thing?"

"Probably not," I answer. Her timing more likely expresses the unique character and personality God created. Her way is not better than other ways. Nor is it worse. It's simply different.

I'm glad I get to be Alyssa's mom. To experience and learn from her outlook, which differs from mine. To be challenged to slow down at Christmas. To enjoy and be grateful.

STOP AND SMELL THE ROSES

Stop and consider the wonderful miracles of God! (Job 37:14 NLT)

Driving with me isn't much fun. I have an extreme type A temperament. You know, the one who's always stampeding toward a goal. In the case of road trips, it means we don't stop often along the way. Coincidentally, I might also be guilty of having a lead foot when cruising down the highway.

I think I've been this way since birth. As the first girl born into the family after four older brothers, I strove to keep up with them at any cost. I remember as a little girl reading the dire warning in *The Poky Little Puppy*. Children's literature aficionados may recall the poky puppy ended up with no dessert at the end of the story. Even without the consequence, I identified with the impatience of the four siblings. As I grew older, my personality matured, and I developed goals and worked toward them with laser-focus. I raced from one activity to another as quickly and efficiently as possible.

Fast forward a few years to my life with Alyssa. She is the human equivalent of the poky little puppy. As the story by Janette Sebring Lowrey goes, five sibling pups would rush out into the world together, but one would always end up missing. The other four would turn around and find him noticing things in life they in their hurry had overlooked. When I read the beloved children's classic to Alyssa, I think her assessment of the poky puppy differed from mine. Out of all the dogs, she felt the most kinship with the slowest moving pup. She had, and still has, one speed for all events in life.

When Alyssa was five years old, we enrolled her in kindergarten. Because we lived a few short blocks from the neighborhood elementary school, we decided to walk there rather than use bus transportation. The school bell rang at nine o'clock, so we left the house in what I thought was plenty of time for the short walk. We stepped off the porch hand in hand. Her new pastel-pink backpack dwarfed her tiny frame. She was so proud of herself.

Pit-pat went her flat-footed gait on the cement sidewalk as her head swiveled to take in all the sights. Cars crawled down the one-way street as boys and girls emerged from their homes. Many children passed us as Alyssa continued to enjoy the crisp autumn air, the birds tweeting from wires overhead, and the burgundy and gold mums adorning many porches along our way. She smiled and called out a cheery "hello" to friends and strangers alike. We were the last of the walkers to arrive at the crossing guard stationed at the bottom of Areba Avenue. Alyssa waved to her as my heart sank. I knew we would arrive late to school on the first day.

"Hurry." My personality kicked into high gear.

"OK," she answered. Her pace remained the same.

We arrived with a flurry of embarrassed excuses from me and a happy smile from Alyssa. "Bye, Mommy." She turned, ponytail swinging, and followed the teacher to her classroom.

I'd like to say I adopted a new attitude immediately. I'd like to say I understood, accepted, even celebrated our personality differences from then on, but I wouldn't be honest. I sometimes need time and repeated experiences to learn.

I accepted trying to hurry Alyssa is like jamming the wrong charging cord into my iPhone. With great force, I can shove the plug into the receptacle, but success means I will damage both the phone and the charger. Because the damage interrupts the power flow, the phone runs out of juice too soon. Out of concern for Alyssa, I learned to slow my walk, to change my expectation of quick replies, and to show patience as she learned. I adapted myself to her needs.

While this change was indeed beneficial, one day, I realized accommodation was not enough.

At Halloween, Alyssa loved dressing in costume to roam the neighborhood, though the free candy was not her main objective. Sweets took a distant second place to the social interaction. In the October dusk, we stepped off our front porch to join hordes of masked kids racing from house to house to fill their buckets to overflowing. Our pace was much more leisurely. We meandered down the street, admiring decorations and visiting with friendly neighbors. Alyssa had trouble walking up and down porch steps, so we took a while to move from one door to the next. The evening culminated with a visit to the house of her kindergarten teacher. Though our Halloween trek was quite short compared to other children in the neighborhood, Alyssa was ecstatic with her sugary plunder. Better still, she always paid off a "mommy tax" in candy bars. She didn't like anything with nuts, so she gave them all to me.

As we left the house, my mind focused on my way of doing Halloween. I preferred to follow the example of those other kids—flying from house to house collecting gobs of chocolate. I matched Alyssa's pace, but inside I champed at the bit. I viewed my way as better. As I observed her, though, a light of understanding dawned on me. Alyssa's way is good. Her ability to notice and enjoy the moment enhanced, rather than impeded, the fun. We don't need to judge between the two options, assuming one is right and the other wrong. Instead, we value the differences. Some folks are go-getters, and some are stop-and-smell-the-roses types. By the end of our excursion, I stopped simply accommodating her perceived limitations and truly accepted her.

In *The Poky Little Puppy*, the title character lingered in one place long enough to use his senses. He heard, saw, and smelled the world around him. In their headlong rush, the four siblings missed out. In the same way, my dash through life had dulled my senses to the world's beauty.

When the canine siblings stopped running to look around for the poky puppy, they discovered their environment—a meadow filled with caterpillars, lizards, frogs, spiders, snakes, and grasshoppers. In the same way, when I pause with Alyssa, the world comes alive. I behold the sparkling dew-soaked flower she bends over to touch. I chuckle at the chattering squirrels chasing one another across the road. I perceive the songbird's melody permeating the still air. I appreciate the smile of the stranger passing by.

God fills his world with wondrous works. He gifted Alyssa with a special ability to break from the pursuit of goals and consider his creation. Thankfully, she's a (mostly) patient teacher in the art of stopping and smelling the roses of life.

A BETTER STORY

Your eyes have seen my formless substance; and in Your book were written all the days that were ordained for me, when as yet there was not one of them. (Psalm 139:16)

"The princess said, 'No! You can't keep me locked up in this tower. My prince is coming. Now!' Then the evil ogre slammed the door shut." Alyssa's childish tones caught my attention as I peeled potatoes for dinner. I smiled and glanced over to see her gesticulating with one chubby hand while the other gripped her picture book. Engrossed in the story, her eyes searched the page. Problem was, she wasn't reading the words. What do you do with a child who'd rather make up her own stories than learn to read what others have written?

At age five, she had not yet begun to read. Oh, we made plenty of efforts to teach her. Preschool and her current kindergarten class laid a groundwork of phonics. She recognized letters. She could create the phonemes of each letter. In my limited experience as a one-time five-year-old, I assumed everyone learned by sounding out words until you became fluent. Yet Alyssa could not string the sounds together to make words. Naïve, I hoped reading would eventually click.

To her advantage, she loved books. She anticipated our daily read-aloud time. She always hung on every word as illustrations and tales grabbed her curiosity. Because of her excellent memory, she knew the stories forward and backward. When I worked with her to sound out words for herself, however, she resisted. I think she found the stories she created from her own imagination to be more interesting and fun than the labor involved with deciphering every word. I took up the challenge to make the author's story worth the effort to read.

Near the end of Alyssa's kindergarten year, I heard about a brand-new book. The title stated its purpose: *Teaching Reading to Children with Down Syndrome: A Guide for Parents and Teachers* by Patricia Logan Oelwein. At a support group I attended, a leader hyped the book as a personalized, visual approach to reading. I couldn't run to the store fast enough. Prior to summer vacation, I read and reread the instructions and created all the resources I would need to employ the recommended methods. I worked my way through a ream of cardstock and rolls of clear adhesive liner to make laminated flash cards, games, and books.

Summer break kicked off my new mission—teaching Alyssa to read. I set aside time every day after work to work with her. The first step was lotto games. The book suggested a list of sight words to memorize. I accomplished the task by matching individual word cards with the same words on a bingo type board as we verbalized them. Using several senses at the same time enhanced her learning and began the process of whole-word recognition. At first, I used vocabulary she already knew—Alyssa, Mom, Dad, and other familiar names. As she succeeded, I moved to other short, common nouns. I chose ones pertinent to her life—dog, cat, book, food items, and the like. When she demonstrated mastery over a group of words, I tested her with flash cards. After much practice, she attained enough sight words for the next step.

I wrote my first book for Alyssa. To engage her attention, I wrote my masterpiece *about* her. I could never be accused of being an artist, so I took photos of Alyssa with things she thought were important. These photos became the illustrations of the story, aptly and unimaginatively titled, *I Like*. I glued them to card stock and wrote a sentence on each page. *I am Alyssa. I like my cat. I like my dog. I like spaghetti. I like my doll.* All these words she had learned using flash cards. To differentiate the words, I wrote each one in a unique color. For durability, I laminated and comb-bound the book.

The day of reckoning arrived. Would Alyssa read, or would she continue to make up her own stories? Anticipation prickled the back of my neck as we opened the book together. I did not read the story to her first, because I had already discovered she has a phenomenal memory. She might simply repeat what she had heard. Instead, I asked her to point to each word from left to right and try to say it.

"What's the first word?" I held my breath as I drew her attention from the picture of herself to the words below.

"I." Hand over hand, we pointed to the next word. "Am." "Alyssa." So far, so good.

"Let's turn the page. What does the next word say?" I asked.

Her stubby middle finger touched the words. "I ... like ... my ... dog."

"Yesss!" She was getting the concept.

Alyssa blinked her wide, blue-flecked hazel eyes at my sudden exuberance. She didn't know she had not been reading before. She didn't realize now she actually was reading. The fascinating story about herself riveted her attention. Success sparked her lifelong love affair with reading.

June melted into July. Alyssa gobbled up new sight words daily. As fast as I could, I made more games to help her recognize common word endings and beginnings. While I can't explain how everything worked in her head, I saw she learned by her own method of decoding new words. By the end of summer, she had learned to read six books I created for her. The literary floodgates burst open.

Today, Alyssa enjoys the thrill of entering other worlds through the door of an author's imagination. She often meanders through far-flung places—Narnia, the Avengers' galaxy, Prince Edward Island with *Anne of Green Gables*, the Swiss Alps with *Heidi*, and Victorian London with *Oliver Twist*. There's no limit to her escapades.

Like Alyssa, I sometimes clamor to create and control my own stunted story. I rely on my imagination framed by my own context rather than allow the Creator to lead me out of my box into his wide and wonderful plans. God is an author who has already written greater adventures for me. When I cede control and submit to his infinite Spirit, I escape my own limited understanding to experience more than I could imagine.

PROVING GROUND

For you know that when your faith is tested, your
endurance has a chance to grow. So let it grow, for when
your endurance is fully developed, you will be perfect
and complete, needing nothing. (James 1:3–4 NLT)

I love sleep, but one year sleep eluded me. I spent
many nights tossing and turning as my mind circled round
and round the events of every day. Poor Jeff felt seasick
clinging to sleep next to me on the sloshing waterbed.

The cause of my angst? First grade. Who knew sending
your child to first grade could be so stressful?

Alyssa had conquered kindergarten. We had planned
and prepared for inclusion. Success followed. Mrs. B
embraced the novel concept of inclusion and welcomed
Alyssa into her classroom. Her positive outlook and
enthusiasm encouraged me.

The summer after kindergarten was also productive.
Alyssa had grasped the concept of reading and developed
a strong foundation for solid reading comprehension.
Gratefully, I looked ahead to the coming school year.

I've always been told in first grade school becomes
more serious. In kindergarten, teachers expect and accept
varying levels of development. In first grade, however,
teachers work to bring everyone up to the same speed,
setting the foundation for the rest of elementary school.

When I sent Alyssa to school in the fall, I prepared myself for some obstacles.

We had already created Alyssa's Individual Education Program (IEP) for the year. The teaching team had agreed on modifications and accommodations for her. She would be in the regular classroom for most instruction but would work with a resource instructor at times for math and reading. The math curriculum emphasized hands-on materials. We scheduled speech and occupational therapy services weekly. We set the strategies for success into place and looked forward to their implementation. With everyone in agreement, and Alyssa eager to begin, we sent her to school.

Alyssa loved school. Unless the weather was bad, and I drove, she strolled there every morning carrying her backpack and lunch. She progressed academically and developed bonds of friendship lasting for years to come. From the lunchroom where she opened her sandwiches to find a mustard happy face on the bread to the playground to special classes like music and art, she reveled in the experience. She was happy.

I still worried. First grade was nothing like kindergarten. Mrs. M's personality did not welcome like Mrs. B. Not overtly friendly, Mrs. M projected a no-nonsense, stern attitude. I concluded, as a more seasoned professional nearing retirement, she preferred not to go out of her way for a special education student included in her classroom. Her minimal communication with me tended toward the negative. Bottom line—I didn't feel very warm and fuzzy about Mrs. M.

I fretted. A lot. At first, concerns dominated my thoughts during the day. Worries plagued me at night. No matter how much self-discipline I exerted, my mind would not shut down. This was uncharacteristic, as I had always been able to zonk out as soon as my head hit the pillow.

Worry often turns into controlling behavior, and mine was no exception. I ramped up my level of involvement in school, so I could note what was going on. I talked to several people on the IEP team. I called the principal. I wondered if I should suggest switching to another teacher. Though a mom should advocate for what's best for her child, I'm sure I sometimes made an unnecessary pest of myself.

By the following spring, I grew exhausted and haggard. I never do well without sleep. I cried out to God. This time, I listened. To his word. To the truth. At the time, I heard a simple song about God's goodness. So simple, the words could be for children. At night, when I lay in bed with worries competing like race cars on an Indy track, I sang this repetitive chorus in my head. I repeated the lyrics until I believed the truth about God, and I fell asleep. If God is good, I can trust him. Completely. With school. With everything. Worry becomes useless when I'm in the hands of a loving, good God.

In the same way first grade sets the foundation for a student, Alyssa's first-grade year formed a foundation in me. This time of intense anxiety was a proving ground for my faith. Merriam-Webster defines a proving ground as "a place where something is developed or tried out." In retrospect, I can see the level of trial was extremely mild, like driving my car over a twig lying in the road. Later in life, I would be depending on God to navigate boulders blocking my way. Yet God used this tiny speed bump in my life to equip me for future roadblocks.

First grade did more than test my faith. It was God's proving ground where he established his trustworthiness to me and expanded my faith and endurance. The following years brought far more difficult experiences into my life, but God's firm foundation never failed.

On those nights when my mind is prone to wander into the wilderness of worry, I still sing myself to sleep with the lullaby of God's goodness. Then I rest like a baby cradled in her daddy's arms.

BOTHERED

How wonderful and pleasant it is when brothers live together in harmony! Harmony is as refreshing as the dew from Mount Hermon that falls on the mountains of Zion. And there the Lord has pronounced his blessing, even life everlasting. (Psalm 133:1, 3 NLT)

The sight warmed the cockles of my heart. Alyssa sat upright in the crook of our sage-and-white-striped sofa. Her short legs dangled over the edge. Her face glowed with pride as she bent over her task, strands of long brown hair swishing across the tightly wrapped bundle cradled in her arm. She touched a bottle to the eager, pursed lips of her baby brother. Mesmerized, I gazed upon them, reveling in the surge of emotion a mother feels when her children show love to one another.

A moment later, Stuart's little round face puckered. His knitted brows scrunched up toward his blond, peach fuzz hair. I knew what would come next. His mouth released the bottle's nipple. A pathetic squall rent the idyllic scene. Alyssa froze, horrified. "Mommy," she wailed. In the cacophony, my heart's cockles cooled considerably.

Such was the roller coaster of sibling life in the Yorty household.

One might think of my pregnancy with Stuart, our second child, as the long, first hill of the roller coaster ride. Months passed as evidence of new life appeared. The specter of a brother became a reality Alyssa could see as my tummy swelled. "My baby," she often said, patting my stomach with soft, pudgy hands and showering him with kisses. Day by day, her anticipation built as she waited to meet him. She had no clue how much life would change.

By age seven, Alyssa relished her well-established position as the only child. In many ways, we behaved as typical first-time parents, jumping to meet every need. Because she has Down syndrome, we devoted immeasurable time to enhancing her development. She basked in the undivided attention of both parents. Like all firstborn kids with a sibling on the way, she was in for a rude awakening.

Stuart's infancy passed with warm, loving moments of butterfly kisses and bear hugs interspersed with brief bouts of bawling and bellowing. As Stuart grew to be a toddler, the twists and turns of the ride changed a bit. A rambunctious two-year old intruded on Alyssa's comfortable world. Bouncy and boisterous, he sprinted headlong into our quiet, methodical life. Inheriting my curiosity gene, he investigated everything. He dove into every part of her life.

"Mommy, Stuart's bothering me!" became Alyssa's constant refrain.

At age three, Stuart insisted on playing tea party with her. Her miniature, pink-flowered tea set didn't stand a chance against his roughshod energy. From the kitchen, I couldn't hear the breakage. Alyssa's shriek and Stuart's trail of blood on the carpet down the stairs first alerted me to the problem. Some pieces from the set remain today as a memento of this now fond memory.

When Alyssa's friend visited for play dates, Stuart refused to be excluded. The girls loved dress-up. Of course, he wanted to join them. While they paraded around in pioneer dresses and bonnets, frilly dance costumes, and evening dresses, Stuart, donned in a Stetson, leather vest, gun belt, and Jeff's cowboy boots, clunked along behind them.

Well before school age, Stuart loved learning. When Alyssa and I worked through lessons at the table, he would sometimes sit and play with the materials. He enjoyed building with her math manipulatives. Other times, he bopped around the room parroting her answers. On some days, he hung on my neck, demanding attention. As one might imagine, all this chaos bothered her quite a bit.

Despite the way Stuart's boundless energy sometimes frayed Alyssa's senses, he also had an uncanny knack for soothing her. The first time he intervened, I stood back, amazed. A minute earlier, she had melted down over math. "I hate adding," she said, throwing her pencil down on the table. "I'm done."

Stuart, busy in his room with LEGOs, must have heard the commotion. Undaunted, he flew down the stairs to her side. He reached up and cupped her round cheeks in his childish palms, drawing her face down to his nose. "Alyssa," he said in his high-pitched Mickey Mouse voice, "you can do this. You need to listen to Mommy." Miraculously, the tantrum subsided, and she meekly retrieved her pencil. Moments like these were the lull before the crazy upside-down part of the ride.

As Stuart grew to adolescence, his childish idolizing of Alyssa diminished. He stopped tagging after his big sister and developed his own interests. Resentment cropped up as she saw him growing in some freedoms she herself had not yet attained. When Stuart learned to drive, she felt excited for him, yet she also more acutely perceived the loss of her own behind-the-wheel aspirations. At times, Stuart was in charge while Jeff and I went out. His authority also bothered her.

Alyssa always points out she is the firstborn child. As a student of the Bible, she knows in Jewish tradition the eldest receives extra inheritance and rights. What she conveniently forgets, though, is those privileges pertain only to males. Nevertheless, she likes to assert her position and expectations. She also believes being born first allows her to plan Stuart's life and boss him around. Not surprisingly, her attitude bothers him, and he doesn't always agree.

Despite her occasional high-handed manner, Alyssa has a soft spot for Stuart. She likes to help him, often offering to fold his laundry. When we're at the store, she wants to buy things for him. If we're visiting a friend and she brings home leftover food, she always asks for a share for Stuart. Though she usually endorses the opposite of what Stuart says, there is one guaranteed time when she takes his side. If Stuart disagrees with me on a matter, she will always back him up. I don't know whether to be annoyed or teary-eyed at their camaraderie.

I love the thrill of roller coasters at the amusement park—tempestuous speed fluctuations, breathtaking mountains and valleys, twirling upside-down and backward, shotgun starts and jerking stops. The roller coasters of this sibling relationship—not so much. As the mom along for the ride, I'd prefer a more sedate experience. I wonder at God's reaction to the way his children often treat one another. I know from his word and from my own experience he is most pleased and honored when we love one another.

My preferences aside, God arranged our family personalities together for his purposes. I see how he is teaching us to submit to one another, wait for gratification, and learn to bear with weaknesses when we're bothered. I doubt our family is unique in this. I suspect, though, in our home the chaos is a bit more exaggerated.

FIT TO BE TIED

God blesses those who patiently endure testing and temptation. Afterward they will receive the crown of life that God has promised to those who love him. (James 1:12 NLT)

"I can't do it, Mom!" The insistent wailing of my daughter twanged my taut nerves on the cold midwinter afternoon. Everything within me silently screamed along with her. *Give up.*

People with Down syndrome usually require intervention with fine motor skills. Alyssa is no exception to this generalization. She has always struggled with fine motor tasks despite years of occupational therapy continuing well into the school setting. By the time she entered second grade, tying shoes still escaped her grasp. Literally.

Yes, I know tying shoes is not a critical life skill. We can make adaptations for those who never master laces. Her life would not be forever ruined if she did not learn to tie shoes, but I wanted to do all I could before consigning her to a lifetime of Velcro. A bit selfishly, I also wanted her to have more independence from me and more options in shoe choices.

As I thought about a solution to this challenge, I applied knowledge I had learned through other experiences with Alyssa. While most people might learn a new task as a whole, she learned best if we broke the skill into smaller parts. Each part could be learned in isolation and later we would meld the skill sets into the whole task. This method had worked before, so I applied it to tying shoes.

The summer before our day of frustration, I analyzed the dreaded task. Little did I imagine how many small skills go into the overall act of tying a shoe. Pull up the tongue. Yank the laces tight. Cross the laces. Bring one lace under the other. Tighten the laces. Make the bunny ear. Run the other lace around. Then the *coup de grâce*, push the bunny through the hole and pull the loop out on the other side to tighten the laces.

For the next step of the process, I consulted with the occupational therapist. She developed various exercises designed to strengthen Alyssa's muscles. For her fingers, we played inchworm on a pencil, twirled straws, picked up and deposited paper clips in a cup, strung pony beads, and pinched wooden clothespins. For the upper arms and shoulder muscles—arm circles, shoulder shrugs, and air punching—across the midline, of course—for bilateral development.

Played may be an overstatement. While I strove to make the exercises fun, they were ... well, not fun. To motivate Alyssa to keep going, I created sticker charts listing all the activities and purchased brightly colored shiny foil stars for her to affix after she had completed the required repetitions of each task. She considered the reward to be a fitting celebration of her accomplishments.

Since September, Alyssa and I had spent thirty minutes every day after school doing the exercises. We also worked on the individual components of tying laces one by one. Our notebook accumulated numerous star-filled pages. Those thirty-minute stretches weren't pretty, but we progressed to the final step by January.

Then we hit the roadblock. Pushing the lace through the hole and pulling it out the other side. Impossible.

I threw up my hands in despair. I was ready to give up. Not necessarily the whole plan, but for one day. Maybe a week. Or perhaps the year. Before my impulse could control me, I remembered an important principle. End on a high note. I had to push through to create a success before we quit for the day.

Let's say Alyssa comes by her stubborn streak honestly, and, yes, maternally. I breathed a prayer for help from God and summoned inner reserves to work on one final, easier task. We managed to end the session with another bright star on the chart.

"Perseverance is the hard work you do after you get tired of doing the hard work that you already did," Newt Gingrich once said. God gifted Alyssa with an abundance of perseverance. She surprises and impresses me with her willingness to continue, albeit sometimes only after a meltdown. I'm certain this quality is the reason she has achieved so much in her life.

In the Bible, James wrote about perseverance for moments like this. Trials and difficulties will, without a doubt, impede progress in life. James asserts if you nevertheless keep striving toward the goal, God gives a reward—a crown of life—to those who love Him. He does not, however, promise life will be easy.

Taking positive steps forward often provides its own reward and motivation to continue working. Even sluggish progress advances the cause. Throughout the fall, Alyssa slogged toward the goal of tying her shoes. The sticker chart, evidence of micro success, inspired her to keep going.

Sometimes we get stuck. Sometimes a challenge shoves us backward, and the next step seems impossible. Clinging to the certainty with God you can keep going, you should push forward toward the goal despite hardship and pain. But on that frustrating day in January, we felt mired, like standing in heavy, hardening cement.

Boy, were we stuck. Nevertheless, we trudged on through thickening discouragement and despair. I wish we had broken through to the big finale right away. Wouldn't the accomplishment be the perfect ending for this story? But this is reality, and we did not. Breakthrough was for another day. God did give us victory over the shoelaces a couple of months later, but not without more tears and much frustration.

Since then, Alyssa has gained independence in tying her own shoes. In the whole scheme of life, shoe tying seems like such an insignificant thing. It's not the biggest deal, but the long process of attaining this small goal became an important lesson in perseverance and has served me well over the years.

COMPARISONS

But they are only comparing themselves with each other, using themselves as the standard of measurement. How ignorant! (2 Corinthians 10:12 NLT)

This will continue until we all come to such unity in our faith and knowledge of God's Son that we will be mature in the Lord, measuring up to the full and complete standard of Christ. (Ephesians 4:13 NLT)

Alyssa seemed to sail through reading. Why not writing? The lament often surfaced in my mind over the years as I labored alongside her teachers to instruct Alyssa in this life-changing skill. Both reading and writing are language-based skills. Her fertile imagination gushed with vibrant stories. What immense barrier lay between her brain and hand blocking thoughts from proceeding through pencil to paper?

Even before kindergarten, Alyssa had been preparing for writing. She had memorized all the letters and their corresponding sounds. This phonics-based approach provides the foundation to acquire reading and writing for most individuals. I later discovered, however, her primary method of learning was different. Nevertheless, she could recognize the letters and produce the correct sounds.

Alyssa also learned to make the shapes of the letters, first with her fingers in fun materials like sand, foam, and rice. Later, she learned to use a writing instrument. First, she traced dotted outlines of letters. Next, she practiced copying letters. Because of limited dexterity in fine motor activities, she could not apply much pressure with the pencil to make well-defined letters. Yet she learned to make a spindly facsimile of the alphabet.

In early elementary school, teachers pushed Alyssa to produce written words and sentences. I'm sure teaching writing involves much more than I understand, but I assumed she, like most kids, would begin writing once given these basic phonics tools. I've seen them put pencil to paper and out pops some semblance of a sentence. Amazing!

Not so for Alyssa. Learning to write was painstaking. In second grade, we realized we needed to separate the mechanics of writing from the content. In other words, give her a way to create sentences and stories without physically writing. We wouldn't give up on the mechanics though. Teachers assigned spelling words, which she scrupulously copied and practiced. She also dictated words and sentences which helpers wrote on paper for her. She later traced over them to practice handwriting.

At periodic parent-teacher meetings throughout the school year, I met with teachers and other paraprofessionals to monitor and discuss progress. Alyssa's growth toward educational benchmarks, though infinitesimal, was measurable and sustained. All agreed she possessed the aptitude for written language, but none offered a real solution to overcome the hurdle blocking the production of writing. Yet we pressed on, trusting one day she would break through.

Spring is IEP season, and we scheduled the final meeting of the year. We intended to update Alyssa's progress and make an educational plan for the coming year. The entire team assembled with me in the conference room at school: speech and occupational therapists, regular and special education teachers, special services director, the teacher's aide, and the principal.

Even in the best of circumstances, IEP meetings often produce stress in parents. I was no exception. While I understood the benefits of the meetings, I always felt what I was building for Alyssa could come crumbling down at a word from another person on the team. I balanced on the tightrope between being a collaborator (aka not asking for too much) and being an advocate.

At this meeting, though, we enjoyed a positive tone. I believe the tension ratcheted down because I had informed the school we were moving to another state before the next school year. They would not assume responsibility for implementing the plan we formulated. First, we brainstormed a list of strengths and needs. Then each professional updated her area of the IEP. All agreed Alyssa had made exemplary academic and social progress. Finally, we created a list of goals for the following year and outlined necessary supports to create success. As the meeting wound down, the tightly coiled spring inside me relaxed. I breathed a sigh of relief as I gathered my papers to leave.

"Oh, Mrs. Yorty," said Mrs. S, Alyssa's regular education teacher, from across the table. "One more thing." She proffered a paper in my direction. "I thought you might like to see an average writing sample from one of the other students in Alyssa's class."

I reached for the paper, which contained a one-page, single-spaced original story written by a typical second grader. Neat, uniform printing covered the page leaving appropriate white space at the margins. The penmanship was something to behold, something for the child who wrote it to be proud of. The narration was leaps and bounds ahead of anything Alyssa had ever produced. Comparatively, her writing was chicken scratch. No offense to chickens.

I held no illusion Alyssa met grade level writing proficiency, so the difference between her samples and this child's work did not surprise me. Yet, the paper in my hand felt like a reality slap in the face.

What could I say? *Why did you hand this to me at the end of the meeting? Did you think I'm unaware of my child's functioning? What is your message? Are you telling me Alyssa doesn't belong in your classroom?* All these thoughts and more cascaded over me like an avalanche.

What did I say? "Thank you." I tucked the paper into my folder as surely as a frightened dog tucks his tail between his legs, and I bolted for the door.

A beautiful, coherent story written by an eight-year-old almost derailed my dreams and convictions about my unique child. I don't think Mrs. S intended to discourage me. I refuse to assign a motive of malice. Alyssa loved her teacher, and I believe Mrs. S cared for her. Yet the comparison she drew to Alyssa's feeble writing attempts stung.

Comparisons cut deep.

I had looked with satisfaction on the slow but steady progress Alyssa made toward successful writing over the past nine months. Until the comparison. Comparisons always leave you feeling less than or more than. Comparisons base evaluations on another person's level rather than evaluations based on an agreed-upon standard. Our wrong human thinking wants to assign inferior and superior positions supported by comparisons.

We have only one standard to worry about, according to Paul in Ephesians 4:13. He puts the focus on Jesus as our standard for achievement and maturity. Of course, I know writing isn't God's main concern here, but this comparison of Alyssa's development turned my heart to a larger truth.

Jesus sets the standard. We, as God's children, pursue his holiness with each step on life's journey. In some stretches, I might sprint. In others, I lag. But fellow travelers shouldn't compete with one another. Instead, each of us should evaluate our progress toward modeling Christ's character, being sure to improve day by day, year after year, toward the goal.

As for Alyssa's writing, I thrust aside the image of the juxtaposed writing samples. The teacher's comparison was at best useless, and at worst, demoralizing. Instead, I focused with gratitude on her perseverance and progress.

BALANCING ACT

Love is patient and kind. (1 Corinthians 14:4 NLT)

But God had mercy on me so that Christ Jesus could use me as a prime example of his great patience with even the worst sinners. Then others will realize that they, too, can believe in him and receive eternal life. (1 Timothy 1:16 NLT)

"I hate this pencil!" Alyssa said, snapping the wood in two.

I didn't witness this incident, but my imagination created the scene when I read the note from Alyssa's third-grade teacher. I was shocked. Not by her frustration, but by the level which drove her to break a pencil. Talk about communication by behavior. Message received, loud and clear.

My heart sank as I lowered into a chair at the kitchen table. I had received more than my share of notes from school. A child with poor communication skills usually finds another, sometimes more obnoxious, way to speak. I knew, or at least hoped, Alyssa would be able to write one day. Were we pushing her too hard?

I struggled with the typical parental dilemma, multiplied by a factor of a hundred for a child with special needs. Sometimes we should not push until a child demonstrates developmental readiness for a particular skill. Some say a child cannot learn until the optimum time. I find merit to this strategy. Children with developmental delays, however, often need nudges—and sometimes shoves—to stimulate the leap to the next level. Parents require great wisdom to walk the line between pushing and patience.

Crazy best described our school year thus far. We had moved to a new state, and Alyssa started third grade in the fall. The school was not thrilled about inclusion for her, but they conceded to her IEP from the previous school. The atmosphere wasn't yet contentious, but tension stretched the bond of cooperation. I think at some level Alyssa perceived the lack of acceptance, but we all tried to make the best of the situation.

Writing became a top priority. Every day, Alyssa practiced at school. After school, she also worked on the task at home. The homework involved writing sentences for eight to ten spelling words. We sat at the kitchen table, and she told me what she wanted to write. I prompted her to verbalize every sound and try to write the letters. We disregarded spelling errors until writing emerged. I championed any connection from brain to paper.

"What is the word you're writing?" I'd say.

"Dog."

"Okay. What's the first sound?"

"Daw," came the answer.

"No, only the first sound. D."

She repeated after me.

"What letter makes the D sound? Can you write it?" Eventually she'd write the correct letter. In this way, we slogged through every letter of every word. (For those who like data analysis, we completed ten sentences with an average of five words per sentence, an average of five letters per word, totaling two hundred fifty letters per night.)

The common scenario would have been tedious enough, but we had a variable that exacerbated the stress. Stuart, an eighteen-month-old toddler at the time, exuded energy and demanded attention. Active, talkative, and climbing, he demanded to be a part of everything his sister did. As I worked with Alyssa, he used me as a human jungle gym. When I asked her for the letter sounds, guess who often said them first?

Some days writing felt like torture. No wonder Alyssa hated the pencil.

Doubts assailed me. This approach was overkill. Should I let writing go? What was the alternative? My questions far outnumbered answers.

So we continued, day after day, week after week, month after month. Alyssa showed a bit of progress in letter formation, but her handwriting remained immature. Some letters were capitals, some were lower case. They often jumped up and down on the lines, spindly and difficult to read. And forget about spelling. I accepted any honest attempt.

One day, though, something clicked. We had completed the dreaded homework, and the smell of dinner wafted from the kitchen. Alyssa traipsed out of the bedroom into the dining room where I was setting the table and handed me a piece of one-inch ruled handwriting paper.

"Look, Mommy." The marks on the page were so light I had to squint in the dwindling, midwinter sun. I snapped on a lamp and peered closer. There I read two complete sentences about Belle from "Beauty and the Beast," one of her all-time favorite stories.

How did this breakthrough happen? I marveled over the two sentences declaring Belle's beauty, as if I held the greatest literary classic in the world, which to me, it was. After all these years of painstaking work, she'd produced this masterpiece without one iota of help. I cried happy tears, and Alyssa beamed in the pride of her accomplishment.

From then on, Alyssa was a writer. Oh, her handwriting continued to be atrocious for several more years, but now she writes legibly. In those days, her awful spelling would have stumped computer spellcheckers. I assumed she'd never become a good speller, but even this skill kicked in when she was a teenager. Now she rarely misspells a word. She wrote many more stories during the school year, and she became pen pals with a friend and a teacher from our previous hometown. I save to this day the very first story she composed.

I wonder ... would Alyssa have written on her own one day without the expenditure of all our blood, sweat, and tears? I have no way of knowing. All I can say is one day the pieces creating the writing process fell into place and flipped the switch of the light bulb. She was ready.

I wonder too ... what does God see in me as he waits for my readiness to grow? Often there's some blockage in the path which I allow to delay my development. Perhaps the hindrance is sin. Or sometimes fear. Often, the sheer stubbornness of wanting to have my way impedes progress. Well, come to think of it, hardheadedness falls into the sin category too. Often, my patient and kind Father waits for my readiness to accept and obey his better way.

At the same time, God also nudges me toward greater holiness. The Bible says he's always preparing us for the next day, the next mission, the next level. Why wouldn't he? He knows where we'll end up and what we'll do, so he shepherds us to our destination. Sometimes I can perceive his still, small voice telling me which way to go, prodding me to step out of my comfort zone to obey. At times, I lean into his directions. Often, though, I'm thickheaded and stubborn. At those times, I'm surprised God doesn't swat me into the next century to get me moving.

My role as Alyssa's mom taught me much about God's perfect balancing act between patience and pushing. Like her, I sometimes melt down, pitch a fit, stomp my feet, and scream in frustration. Such behavior doesn't often appear on the outside since I'm more mature, but God knows everything going on inside. Yet his patience and kindness far exceed anything I can ever demonstrate to Alyssa. I'm thankful through her I can better understand my Father's kind heart.

UNSHAKABLE

I have set the Lord continually before me; because He is at my right hand, I will not be shaken. (Psalm 16:8)

ASSUME = ASS + U + ME

The military sometimes has a unique way of expressing truths. Long ago as a teenager in Civil Air Patrol, I learned a saying about the word *assume*. When you assume, you make an ass out of you and me. In other words, get your facts straight before acting on first impressions.

Assumptions abound about individuals with Down syndrome. Nearly all are false. Most people have no real experience interacting with a person who is blessed with an extra twenty-third chromosome, so I never expect too much. I did anticipate educational professionals, particularly those with expertise in teaching exceptional children, would have a broader understanding of the wide range of possibilities.

In my experience, many do not. Right before Alyssa entered third grade, we moved to North Carolina. I transferred the education plan developed with the prior school to provide a starting point for the new teacher. Upon arrival in our new home, I called the special education department to enroll.

"Oh, she has Down syndrome. She'll be in the resource classroom," the official said to me.

"How does the placement work?" I asked, suspicious of her quick (and illegal) assumption.

"She'll get most of her education in the special ed room, and she'll be mainstreamed for specials like art and music."

Alyssa had never learned in this type of setting before, and its restrictions did not support our overall vision for her life. "She has an IEP calling for inclusion in a regular ed classroom," I said. "I understand we must start with a placement there."

After a moment of awkward silence, the administrator scheduled our first IEP meeting. Meanwhile, Alyssa's placement would be at our local school in a classroom with her age-appropriate peers.

Thus commenced a two-year odyssey (aka nightmare) with a school district with no desire to implement inclusion. They remained unmoved by the fact Alyssa had five years of successful inclusion prior to their school. They had never tried inclusion for someone with Down syndrome, and they weren't about to attempt it with her.

The school complied with the necessary legal requirements. Officials placed Alyssa in a regular classroom with the supports specified by her IEP, but the school psychologist scheduled her for aptitude and achievement testing. They discovered what I already knew. Her achievement scored higher than her IQ indicated. By the middle of fall, the school disregarded achievement and moved to change the placement based on her IQ score.

I followed the system set in place by the special education law, Individuals with Disabilities Education Act, to block the scheduled transition to another classroom and to negotiate an agreeable path forward. Alyssa needed more evaluations, this time at Duke University. There I found an expert and ally who taught me much about Alyssa's educational strengths and weaknesses. Her support through the process proved invaluable.

Managing Alyssa's education grew into a full-time job. I filled reams of paper with copious notes taken during school meetings galore. I scaled a huge learning curve researching resources and supports with burgeoning internet technology. Constant phone calls left my ear burning. I grew adept at managing a toddler and a household while talking or waiting on hold.

I worked hard to affirm and support Alyssa's classroom teacher as well. For obvious reasons, I tried to maintain a good working relationship with the one who influenced my child for most of every day. To achieve my goal, I heeded any communication sent home and ensured Alyssa completed assignments. Through all the uncertainty, I strove to lift her above the tension so she would maintain a positive attitude toward school.

The school continued to push for a segregated classroom. At the IEP meeting near the end of third grade, they got their way. Seated as one of many around a large conference table at the school district office, I could not stop the team's new placement recommendation—resource classroom.

The battle did not end there. If I wanted inclusion for Alyssa, I would need to pursue due process. Jeff and I scraped together enough money to hire an attorney for the required legal proceeding. I prayed the case could be resolved before going to court because I knew our retainer wouldn't last long. The school's financial pockets went far deeper than ours. We continued to hope for a reasonable negotiation.

Because I filed for due process, Alyssa's fourth grade began under the IEP stipulating inclusion. Stress mounted as our case moved forward. Though she was unaware of the educational melee, tension pervaded her classroom like dark clouds overshadowing a picnic. Her outlook toward learning deteriorated. Too stubbornly, I clung to the belief the school and I could come to a meeting of the minds.

The legal wrangling and the year dragged on. With other options exhausted, the court scheduled a mediation hearing for midwinter. Unfortunately, our ability to pay for legal counsel ran out prior to hearing. Representation at the hearing cost money we didn't have. I would have to go alone.

The weeks leading up to mediation were frenzied. Alongside my normal responsibilities, I now put on my attorney hat to prepare for the unknown. Years earlier, I had worked as an administrator in a law firm, so at least I had a modicum of familiarity with the legal system. That— and the gavel inscribed "Judge Yorty" I had received as a parting gift. My chance of success was slim. Nevertheless, I expended my best effort, assembling a mountain of documents and outlining my negotiating strategy.

Anxiety became my constant companion in the days leading up to the hearing. I pictured myself sitting all alone at the mediation table across from the school's army and a judge at the head. Who would sit by my side to advocate for me?

The night before the hearing, I searched God's Word, longing for encouragement. For hope. God led me to a word in Psalms which leaped off the page right into my circumstance. "He is at my right hand. I will not be shaken." *What?* I read the words again, letting the promise sink in. God is by my side as an advocate.

The next day, I marched into the mediation room pulling a small suitcase of documents all categorized and labeled. After unloading and organizing, I settled into a chair on my side of the table, glancing to my right. Though the seat was empty, I sensed I was not alone.

Not only was God with me in the hearing, but he also gave me favor. I presented evidence to support my case, and the mediator agreed Alyssa should be educated in a regular classroom setting. The school district decided not to pursue the matter further. She spent the rest of the year in her usual classroom, and we created a good plan to provide for her needs going forward.

Waging a two-year battle over Alyssa's educational rights drove me to the end of my strength and resources. In fact, the struggle carried me all the way to the end of myself. Running out of yourself is a good thing, though gut-wrenching. My hopeless, desperate moment prodded me to invite God to step in and show me more of his character. More of his presence. More of his provision.

He cannot and did not fail. Because of God's faithful presence, I will never be shaken.

COURSE CHANGE

"My thoughts are nothing like your thoughts," says the Lord. "And my ways are far beyond anything you could imagine. For just as the heavens are higher than the earth, so my ways are higher than your ways and my thoughts higher than your thoughts." (Isaiah 55:8–9 NLT)

You want me to do what now? The fact I didn't vocalize the words did not minimize my utter shock. I was so certain of my course. Now my GPS, God's Positioning System, told me to take the sharp turn ahead. Surely its signal got confused.

I had laser-focused for more than seven years on educational inclusion for Alyssa. Over the past two years, I had burned through countless hours fighting for her right to be in the regular classroom in public school. I had, in fact, won my case in legal due process. How in the world could God be leading me to abandon inclusion in favor of homeschooling?

Yes, I had entertained the idea of homeschooling earlier in the year when the prospect of winning my case against the school system appeared dismal. I settled on pulling Alyssa out of school as my if-all-else-fails plan. I never considered home to be the ideal place for her to learn. When due process succeeded, I discarded the notion without regret.

Still, the conviction to homeschool nagged at me every day. Summer break ushered in a time of reevaluation. As I analyzed the year after winning at mediation, I realized I danced on pins and needles. Trying to make sure Alyssa's needs were met. Trying to stay on track with the academics and behavior. Trying to keep the teacher happy. All in hope the school would want to include her.

The light of truth clarified the situation. If the school bought into the idea of inclusion, they would promote success. Conversely, if they didn't want Alyssa in the regular classroom, they could cause her to fail. We'd wind up back in IEP meetings hashing out the same issues again. Of course, I could push back every time, but what would the endless cycle do to her?

Homeschooling, though, seemed to be the antithesis of inclusion—the most, not least, restrictive environment— everything I had rejected in the past. I also worried I was ill-prepared to teach Alyssa. I wondered how her need for social interaction could be met. I based all my concerns on assumptions rather than true knowledge. Yes, I do remember what ASSUME means.

I recalled all I had learned so far in this journey with Alyssa. Down syndrome? Check. Teaching to read? Check. The legal system? Check. Writing? Well, she learned to write, but I had no idea how. I decided writing deserved a check too. God had prepared me for each challenge along the way.

I embraced the route recalculation and dug into homeschooling. The more I read, the more I could see possibilities for Alyssa. One useful book outlined different learning styles and motivations. She learned best when she could show or perform her work, so I searched for curricula designed for her style. Instead of using a comprehensive homeschooling program, I selected individual subject materials. To capitalize on her reading aptitude, I filled my shelves with literature-based options including lots of visuals and repetition. This also gave me a handy excuse to feed my book addiction.

As for social opportunities, we lived in an area where homeschooling popularity exploded. I joined up with a few friends at church to begin a support group. The number of families multiplied. Every week, we shared the responsibility of teaching cooperative classes. We visited many historical sites, museums, and businesses as we crisscrossed the state for field trips. For fun, we seized every opportunity to create educational festivities. Of course, we held the usual major holiday events. We also celebrated influential figures such as Martin Luther King, Jr., Saint Valentine, Susan B. Anthony, Saint Patrick, and Sacagawea.

Alyssa flourished in the homeschooling environment. Because I could tailor studies to her specific strengths and vary the pace as necessary, she achieved new concepts and skills. She also enjoyed relationships with peers, participating in less-competitive sports, music, dance, and theater. Dance and theater were, and still are, among her favorite activities. To tie the academics all together, I wove threads of service to God and community throughout the fabric of everyday life.

While I appreciated the many benefits of homeschooling Alyssa, I bought them at a steep price. Time. Money. Creativity. Energy. Emotions. Pressure. The weight of responsibility pressed daily upon my shoulders. I experienced inclusion challenges too. When she joined groups for learning, I often needed to educate parents, modify materials, and monitor results. Success demanded significant creativity and commitment on my part.

My first year of homeschooling hooked me. Learning new things alongside Alyssa jazzed the lifelong learner in me. The ability to flex according to the demands of life freed me. Dreaded IEP meetings were now a reflection in the rearview mirror. As a side benefit, I loved not getting up super early in the morning.

But all those perks could not sustain me for the long haul. Homeschooling demanded a deeper motivation. I could never maintain the level of commitment required year after year based only on dislike of the public school system. I needed a conviction. A calling.

Weary by the end of the first year, I signed up for a summer homeschool conference. There I learned about operational matters—techniques, curricula, and reporting. I also received fellowship and encouragement. Others who were farther down the path than I turned back to share their vision, their struggles, and their joys. Every year after the first conference, I nourished myself with such inspiration.

Back in the early days when homeschooling was a glimmer shining through my public-school tunnel vision, doubts assailed me. Then God brought a short Bible verse to my attention. "Faithful is he who calls you, and he also will bring it to pass" (1 Thessalonians 5:24). This promise scrolled across my computer screensaver as a reminder of God's faithfulness throughout my sixteen years of homeschooling. Its truth still reverberates in my heart today.

PURE JOY

For by grace you have been saved through faith; and this is not of yourselves, it is the gift of God; not a result of works, so that no one may boast. For we are His workmanship, created in Christ Jesus for good works, which God prepared beforehand so that we would walk in them. (Ephesians 2:8–10)

The room darkened. The audience hushed. A dull thud of footsteps echoed from behind the hollow stage as dancers rushed to their positions. The breath lodged in my throat as I glanced yet again at the program, now impossible to read. I already knew Alyssa would be next. Eager anticipation and nerves rose together in my chest.

By the time Alyssa turned eight or nine years old, I had figured out she learns kinesthetically. She internalizes information by experiencing things. She understands best when she can touch, move, or even act out the content of lessons. As a mom and teacher, I strove to provide lots of active kinesthetic opportunities to cement concepts. This led us to dance.

Dance was new territory for me. As a one hundred percent-tomboy kid, I played every kind of sport with my brothers. Had I been offered the chance to participate in dance, I would have sprinted in the opposite direction as fast as my short legs could carry me. Nevertheless, I charted foreign waters and located a dance studio for Alyssa.

An explosion of femininity greeted us on the night of the first lesson. I blinked at the pastel walls and mirrors. Lithe teenage dancers attired in black leotards and tights slipped in and out of classrooms with ballet slippers and pointe shoes dangling over their shoulders. Younger ballerinas dressed in frilly pink tutus and sparkly soft footwear pranced about, giggling in excitement. Thankfully, I had garnered enough dance knowledge to attire Alyssa appropriately for her lesson. As we took a seat in the lobby to wait, she gazed in awe. This was her world. These were her people.

After she joined her group, I watched through one-way glass with apprehension. I didn't know what to expect. How would Alyssa respond to the structure of the classroom? Would she be able to keep up with the other dancers? Would her teacher understand her speech? Would she accept Alyssa?

Miss Angie displayed beauty, patience, and kindness to her students. Alyssa gravitated to her sweet nature, but she loved dancing even more. Dance practices over the course of the year had ups and downs. Because of her natural flair for choreography, Alyssa enjoyed collaborating with the other students to create movements to match the music and words. She did not have much patience, however, for repeating a particular section of the routine over and over to achieve perfection. In her mind, practicing the entire dance from beginning to end without interruption made more sense. Despite this, her enthusiasm for dance never waned.

We found Alyssa's *raison d'être*—her reason for being—and her lifelong joy.

Alyssa has been involved in dance in one way or another ever since Miss Angie's class so many years ago. After we moved from North Carolina to Kentucky, she was talking with her friend Rainey one Sunday at church when the topic of dance came up. Rainey and Alyssa hatched a plan to begin a dance ministry. The team blessed the church on many occasions with their expressive worship of God. When we moved to Pennsylvania, she continued her involvement with dance. She chooses songs and creates beautiful individual routines for performance at churches and talent shows. Some days, I hear music and peek into her bedroom to find her attired in a pastel-pink leotard, dancing her heart out for an audience of One.

Alyssa has participated in other creative outlets as well. She sang for several years in an inclusive group of kids aged six to sixteen. The leaders accepted every person at every level of ability and encouraged them to perform solos. Each year, they learned an entire slate of new songs they performed at venues all over the state. She sang on the steps of the capitol, at a Philadelphia Eagles football game, baseball games, festivals, churches, parks, and patriotic celebrations.

She also joined a Christian musical theater group for a few years. A born actress, Alyssa memorizes lines with just one reading and possesses a knack for the dramatic. Not surprisingly, she sometimes thought she knew better than the director, but on performance days she always delivered. She doesn't do much acting nowadays, but she still writes her own scripts and stories.

Horseback riding provides another outlet for Alyssa's showmanship. I'll never forget her first horse show—a tiny six-year-old atop a giant, sleek brown steed, maneuvering him through an obstacle course. As her body flopped with the horse's gait, her grin could not have stretched wider. Yet when she received her first ribbon, somehow her smile beamed even brighter. She still rides to this day.

As an adult, Alyssa derives much satisfaction and meaning from singing in the church choir. Her pitch may not always be perfect, but her heart tunes to God as she belts out her worship.

We're all created to bring glory to God. How his majesty manifests is as unique as everyone's personality and gifting. God did not make Alyssa love math, excel at sports, wield power, or eat green beans. These things do not bring her joy. Creative performance is her special opportunity to shine and to connect with God.

I saw a change come over Alyssa when she put on her first dance performance costume—a sparkly purple number with a skirt that swished when she moved. A light touch of makeup and a tightly secured bun wrapped in ribbon accentuated her animated face. I sensed no nervousness in her. Somehow, those nerves all lodged in the pit of my stomach, frenzied butterflies beating a tattoo against my rib cage. She pranced away from me to join her group as I found my seat in the auditorium.

The lights burst onto the stage as I shifted to the edge of my chair anticipating my girl's performance. A gentle melody accompanied the girls as they twirled, dipped, and swayed, arms wide with graceful fingers outstretched as if a tiny bird were perched there. Toes pointed, they leaped for joy. Alyssa's face glowed with pleasure at doing what she was made to do. The breath seeped out of my lungs as my heart burst with pride. All too soon the dance ended, and the auditorium erupted in applause. I leaped to my feet, tears streaming down my cheeks, whooping and hollering for my girl.

A BETTER WAY

I will ask the Father, and He will give you another Helper,
so that He may be with you forever. (John 14:16)

Weeping. Gnashing of teeth. A head banging against the desk. All from me.

Such was the daily math agony with Alyssa. Our dependable *Math-U-See* curriculum had mutated into "Math-Makes-Tears." Though she never excelled at math, her lessons had not always tortured us in this way.

Math instruction started in her toddler years with early intervention. We touched and counted everything from blocks, stairs, sidewalk squares, blueberries, crayons, and much more. We sorted shapes and matched them over and over. We searched for patterns everywhere in the world around us and organized items by size. To prepare for sequence and spatial relationships which undergird math concepts, we practiced a list of positional words such as over, under, and behind. With games as the primary means of learning, we had fun—mostly.

In kindergarten, I could see Alyssa's weakness in math more clearly. She struggled with one-to-one correspondence—counting each object in a set only once—while other children were already grouping objects and counting by twos or tens. While they could look at a small set of objects and recognize how many, she still touched and counted to find the number. Nevertheless, she progressed.

Through the elementary years, Alyssa's IEP always reflected her needs in math. Yet she mastered concrete and representational concepts. Teachers introduced her to a curriculum with a strong visual connection between numerals and the quantity they represent. The multisensory approach appealed to her learning style. This method advanced through addition, subtraction, and multiplication.

I suspected Alyssa's indelible memory would serve her well in memorizing math facts. I hoped even if she struggled with the concepts of operations, she might use rote facts in practical circumstances. To achieve rote results, we studied flash cards and practiced equations daily. The effort ended in abysmal failure. Let's say I have now proven without a shadow of a doubt her brain is not wired to remember numbers. Yet, due to her tenacity, she eventually could recite addition, subtraction, and multiplication tables in order. Despite her achievement, random recall and on-the-fly application of these facts remained difficult.

Homeschooling opened a new world of curriculum choices, and I found *Math-U-See*. Alyssa enjoyed certain aspects of this multisensory approach. I also decided, since we had given math facts a strenuous attempt, she could now use a calculator for computation. I always worked one-on-one with her, providing manipulatives and verbal prompts for problem-solving, so she continued to grow in knowledge.

In this slow and steady way, Alyssa progressed to algebra, where the steps in the processes grew lengthier. Then things went downhill like an inverse parabola. For all you non-math majors, picture a curve shaped like a steep mountain. When she had trouble remembering all the steps, I hatched the brilliant idea to create written algorithms. Algorithm is a fancy word for a flowchart. I first presented the simpler problems, and, in a fit of optimism, I also wrote algorithms for the more complicated if/then situations. I aspired to at least partial mathematical independence for her.

I taught her how to use these charts. Our usual dialogue went something like this:

> **ME:** "Okay, Alyssa, what's the first step? Read it from the list." She reads the direction out loud.

> **ME:** "Good. Now let's follow it." She looks down at the notebook paper and writes the numbers. I see they're out of alignment.

> **ME:** "Here, let's turn the paper sideways and stay in the lines." She flips the paper and writes the numbers again where I am pointing.

> **ME:** "Okay, what's the second step?" She accidentally skips the step when she's reading aloud.

> **ME:** "No, you missed step two. Let's use a piece of cardboard to cover the other words so we don't get ahead of ourselves."

I remind myself I need to make copies of this algorithm with spaces to check off each item as she goes.

> **ALYSSA:** "Look, Mom, there's a red bird outside."

My momentary lapse into thought provides an opportunity for her distraction.

> **ME:** "I see. Let's pay attention now. What's the next step?"

Alyssa holds the cardboard in place and scrutinizes the algorithm. She reads the instruction aloud. "Now use the calculator to figure it out." With great deliberation, she mashes the buttons. When a number pops up, she begins to write what she sees. When I notice a wrong answer, a silent scream rips through my mind.

> ME: "You must have pressed the wrong buttons. Let's try again."

She wails in frustration and erases the mistake, taking out some of the previous numbers. Rather than make her start over, I take her pencil and rewrite the obliterated numerals. She reworks the calculator and writes the answer.

> STUART: "Mom, can I ...?"

I cut him off (probably not so nicely) because I see Alyssa's head whip up from her painstaking work.

> ME: "Not now, Son. We need total silence. Alyssa, you still need to write what it says on the calculator."

We look down to find the digital display is cleared. I punch in the numbers again and she copies them.

> ME: "Look back at the card and find your place."

By now, the cardboard has been bumped and no longer shows which line to read. She jumps to step number six.

> ME: "Errrggg!"

Commence teeth gnashing and head banging.

This is a small testimonial for my "Math-Makes-Tears" curriculum. You're compelled to run out and buy your own copy, right? Believe it or not, we slogged all the way through algebra by the end of the year. At the end, after hiding in a corner to suck my thumb when the math lesson finished day after day, I admitted defeat. I found a consumer math curriculum to complete the required math credits. While the program wasn't easy, the real-world application made more sense to her than algebra.

This little life vignette taught me an important lesson. I can see myself in Alyssa's shoes, trying so hard to follow God's rules to get things right. I long for an algorithm, a list of exact steps to follow so I won't get off track. Take parenting, for example. Wouldn't we be better off with a list of if/thens? When your kid does this, you do that. When she says "A," you say "B." But life doesn't work that way. We cannot write a formula for every situation.

Instead, God gives me his principles in the Bible, and he provides a helper to apply them in every situation. With God's Spirit, life's algorithm is simple: Things happen. Listen to the Spirit. Do what you're told.

I'm sure God's Spirit doesn't experience the emotional rollercoaster I rode with Alyssa. He stays by my side, guiding me one-on-one when I'm distracted. Frustrated. Copping a bad attitude. Even when I'm disobedient. Abject failure with our nemesis, algebra, demonstrated to me algorithms will never be the best solution for life. God provides a far better way. If I follow the leading of the Spirit, I'll abandon the flowcharts and take the next step in life.

CREATED FOR GLORY

As He passed by, He saw a man blind from birth. And His disciples asked Him, "Rabbi, who sinned, this man or his parents, that he would be born blind?" Jesus answered, "It was neither that this man sinned, nor his parents; but it was so that the works of God might be displayed in him." (John 9:1–3)

Blindsided.

My knees buckled under me one warm spring evening when Alyssa dropped a bombshell. It exploded in the middle of an already difficult conversation about assessing people by outward appearances. She told me how a negative assumption about her abilities had stung her tender heart, leaving her confused and hurt, dehumanized by a judgment based on her group identity. She struggled to find value in herself as a person with Down syndrome.

I paused to consider how to acknowledge the reality of others' views of Down syndrome while retaining her dignity and positive self-worth. As I formulated a gentle answer in my mind, Alyssa said, "Oh, it's like how people think babies with Down syndrome should be aborted."

Boom! Her grenade sent me reeling, mouth hanging slack with no good answer. Through the open window, birds nesting for the night chirped into the stunned silence.

How could I answer her question? She is correct. The reasons for termination vary. Raising a child with a disability causes severe hardship. The child will suffer. She'll never contribute to society, only taking away limited resources from other, more deserving individuals. Healthcare will be a financial strain. Maybe she would be better off not living. We should try again for a "normal" child. Such arguments may seem sound in times of doubt and fear.

In fact, a vast majority of women with a prenatal diagnosis succumb to this reasoning. Statistics show almost seventy percent of expectant mothers in the United States choose to terminate pregnancy when confronted with the possibility of Down syndrome. Many European countries' rates soar much higher, ranging up to ninety percent. In the extreme, in 2017, Iceland boasted of all but eliminating Down syndrome through prenatal testing and termination.

If you're one of the shrinking number of people whose peers are planned for extinction, what is the effect on your psyche? Your identity? How do you thrive in a world where others view you as less than? Alyssa does not answer these questions, but that day I realized knowledge of the truth of abortion had impacted her identity. She connected the grim reality to how people perceive and value her.

Others constantly judge Alyssa by the "wrapper" of Down syndrome. When people interact with her, they draw conclusions based on her appearance and obvious diagnosis. Some assume benign positive attributes. Down syndrome children are so loving. They always want to hug. They are always so happy. Other pernicious stereotypes cut to the quick. These children are stubborn. They can't speak. People with Down syndrome drain society's resources.

Alyssa recognizes her inferior status in the stares and whispers. She knows by the fact people often speak past her to me. Most hold low expectations for the future of individuals with Down syndrome. When she was eight years old, a teacher told me she should aim for a job sweeping up hair in a beauty salon. I'm not denigrating the importance of any job, but we don't usually designate such a career for a person at a young age.

Alyssa aches when schools and church groups fail to accept her. She wishes for more and varied work opportunities. She mourns the absence of normal things most people take for granted. She'll never possess a driver's license. She squelches a natural longing to marry and have children. Sometimes to her detriment, people give her a pass on all misbehavior because they suppose she can't do any better. All these and more remind her of the world's derogatory opinion of people with Down syndrome.

God created every one of us. Perfection himself, he makes no mistakes. At a deep level, I recognized this fact as the source of the only answer which would satisfy Alyssa's heart-wrenching declaration. Though God fashions unique individuals, most fall within certain norms. Some, however, God designs differently. Though the world often designates these specially gifted folks as "the least of these," God plans a good purpose for their lives. Jesus himself revealed the reason. God wishes to display his works, even his glory, through individuals like Alyssa.

God also desires every individual would come to know him. Every person he created possesses the ability to connect at a heart level with him. He leaves no one outside of his promises. God has been faithful to Alyssa. He called her into relationship with him when she was nine years old, and he showcases his glory in her life. He endowed her with the ability to sense him in ways I do not always understand. She has joined his beautifully varied orchestra as an instrument filling the world with strains of his grace.

You may know someone who decided not to bear a child and now regrets her choice. How might Alyssa respond to her? I suspect she would first utter a dramatically horrified gasp. She might even wag a finger. She would look the woman in the eye and tell her straight up, "You shouldn't have aborted your baby." After a hug, she'd suggest going for chocolate chip cookie dough ice cream together. That's Alyssa.

To my knowledge, she does not dwell on the world's perception of her differences. Yes, some days I see she is frustrated, but these thoughts don't seem to consume her. I value friends who see her as God intended. As her mom, I know I am privileged to have a front row seat for the show of God's glory displayed through her life.

GOD'S EMBRACE

Sing for joy, O heavens! Rejoice, O earth! Burst into song, O mountains! For the Lord has comforted his people and will have compassion on them in their suffering. (Isaiah 49:13 NLT)

I slumped to the kitchen floor, shaking as sobs racked my body. My kids slept in their beds, and Jeff worked the night shift. Earlier in the day, rejection had smashed my heart. At the time, I scooped its shattered pieces into a box and held myself together. Until now. Finally alone, I allowed the clasp on the box to snap. Anguish poured out in unrelenting tears and wails I couldn't stifle. I ached for my daughter.

I had been volunteering at school. "I can't wait for my birthday party on Saturday," Alyssa's friend said as she skipped over to me.

"I'm coming," Alyssa said, confident of her invitation. "Mom, we need to get a present."

"No …" her friend answered, "I'm having only a few friends for a sleepover. Maybe you can come later." Confusion, disappointment, and anger flashed across Alyssa's round face. I redirected her attention before her emotions exploded in impulsive, fiery words.

Rejection comes from strangers, coworkers, friends, and even family. Often, it takes the form of a thoughtless comment or a move away from the closeness of the relationship. Sometimes, the rebuff is a polite "maybe she'd do better elsewhere." Other times, the brush-off is much more blatant. Yes, I told myself, everyone experiences rejection. Alyssa is not alone, but exclusion of a child at any age crushes a mama's heart. With each rejection, I must decide. Do I help her persist and pursue reconciliation? Or do I guide her to accept the snub and move on?

I can blow off the disdain of a stranger. I ignore the extra-long stares. Other times, people assume Alyssa can't speak. She never hesitates to overcome that one for herself. Many underestimate her abilities. I understand. People may not know any better. Though I get this, some days, even these small things pile up.

Rejection from friends slices much deeper. Exclusion happens often during teen years when everything changes, almost daily. Most adolescents experience insecurity as they struggle to understand themselves and the world around them. They make lots of mistakes. Friendships come and go at lightning speed amid teenage uncertainty. For a young person, accepting someone like Alyssa who is different may endanger their place of belonging in the crowd.

Alyssa entered this time of life along with her friends at a nearly equal level of maturity, but a disparity emerged as they gained independence she had not yet attained. Peers who played higher-level sports gravitated to friends who shared their affinity. Some took jobs and diverted energy from relationships. She didn't blend in at many teen parties, so friends often excluded her. How could I help her understand she can't go to a party to which she hasn't been invited? Better question—how do I explain why she wasn't invited? Whatever the reason, friends' once parallel paths now separated. Alyssa's way was much less traveled. She suffered through the angst of these losses, and my mother's heart grieved along with her.

Church and other Christian groups also became less welcoming and accommodating for Alyssa in her teen years. At youth groups, few went out of their way to draw her into social activities outside of Sunday mornings. She tried attending Christian clubs boasting acceptance of all kids, regardless of where they were in their spiritual journey. Their convictions did not include embracing an outspoken girl with intellectual challenges.

Particularly gut-wrenching was the lack of acceptance by Christians—my brothers and sisters called by God to promote belonging and inclusion in his family. Every time we moved to another region, over and over, we endured this hurt. The rejections were more subtle, diplomatic.

"Maybe this isn't the right place for Alyssa." *Because she doesn't need God?*

"I'm not sure we can accommodate her needs at this camp." *Why won't you try?*

"She may not feel comfortable at this party." *Being left out is even more uncomfortable.*

"We don't do that type of ministry." *Shouldn't you be?*

In these situations, I often try to get ahead of problems by easing concerns the person or organization might feel. People have questions, anxiety, or even fear because they may not have experienced a person with Down syndrome. I share information about Down syndrome and Alyssa's particular needs, inviting them to ask any questions. Though doing this puts me far outside my comfort zone, I suck up my insecurities and risk myself, asking, "Will you please accept my daughter?" In the end, some answer "no," usually couched in nice Christian terms. Often, the place where people should extend belonging to all isn't interested in "that type of ministry."

Some people cower and slink away when rejected. I'm more likely to attempt to assert rights. Advocacy is appropriate in certain situations, but in relationships, you can't force acceptance. Someone is either willing—or not. I must make judgments about the value of pressing forward in attempts to change hearts and minds. Did the comment or decision come from a place of misunderstanding? We can probably resolve it. Or did the slight come from resistance? If so, I've learned to cut my losses when the other person is not inclined to accept.

I reasoned, like everyone, Alyssa must undergo and even grow from inevitable rejection. Unlike the experience of most teens, however, people often filtered rejection of her through me. Sometimes the blow walloped me. Knocked me flat. Once I stood up again, I took responsibility to deliver the heart-rending message to Alyssa. What mom wants to be the instrument of rejection time and again? Yet I'm grateful for the opportunity to try to shield her from the brunt of exclusion.

My best strategy? Refocus. On what, or whom, would I choose to fix our attention? Sometimes rejection enveloped my mind and emotions in a cloud so thick I couldn't perceive anything else. Pain and confusion overwhelmed and disoriented me. I forgot about the good in life. I failed to notice the ones who accepted and loved Alyssa. When I deliberately and doggedly reminded myself of God's blessings, though, my head popped above the dense fog into the sunlight of gratitude.

Indeed, God gave Alyssa many friends in her circle of acceptance. Of course, she has extended family who love her. For years after we moved to a new state, she also corresponded with a pen pal from elementary school.

Another girl known from childhood went to camps with her and remains her friend today. Many organizations accept and value her volunteer contributions. People in our church small groups take the time to get to know her and engage with her. In every place we've lived, God provided some who treasure Alyssa.

I'm convinced relationships are messy for everyone. The other individual may choose not to put in the effort to cultivate a connection. Sometimes a season of close friendship ends because of life transition. Even those with the best intentions occasionally cause pain.

Many verses in the Bible remind us to fear only God. His word says do not worry about the approval of those around us. Yet the execution of this simple command proves difficult. God created humans for fellowship, to extend hearts to friends, family, and even strangers. But we assume a huge risk to open our soft, vulnerable spot to another person, giving them the power to wound with arrows poisoned with rejection. When—not if—exclusion happens, it's difficult to brush off. Rejection clings like cat hair on cashmere. Being scorned often looms larger than the knowledge of God's eternal love and acceptance.

Curled on the cold tile that evening surrounded by shards of my heart, I wrapped my arms around my body, a feeble attempt at self-comfort. It didn't work. "Why?" I asked God. "Why is this life so hard?" There was no audible reply. Instead, I felt the warm embrace of God's Spirit as he reminded me even he experiences rejection. I dried my swollen eyes and rose once again. Perfect acceptance for Alyssa, and for me, is found in God alone.

NEW AND IMPROVED

Behold, I am going to do something new, now it will
spring up; will you not be aware of it? I will even make
a roadway in the wilderness, rivers in the desert. (Isaiah
43:19)

"Maroon and white. Go Madison County!" The shout,
accompanied by rhythmic clapping and foot stomping,
resounded throughout the gym. A spotlight found seven
young ladies in identical pleated skirts and tops, swinging
ponytails adorned with maroon and white ribbons. In the
audience, I mouthed the words as my muscle memory
mirrored every move of the routine. Alyssa's cheer team
put on a flawless performance.

This delightful moment and many more like it almost
didn't happen.

Why? Because the cheerleading team was part of
Special Olympics. Still confused? So was I.

My mind fixated on inclusion. Total inclusion—Alyssa
doing every activity with typical peers. Because of this
goal, we exposed her to many sports activities from an
early age. Her first soccer experience came at age five.
Every Saturday morning in autumn, she and other kids
chased a wayward ball across dew-soaked grass like
a prize in a candy scramble. She focused little on the
strategy of the game, but over the years, she continued to
play and enjoyed participating with her friends.

Alyssa also played T-ball. If you ask me, she was the cutest baseball player out of all the kids digging in the dirt of the base path, picking flowers in the outfield, and running the wrong way. She also learned the rules of dodgeball and kickball and ran relay races. Basketball was rough, since even as a grown person, she stands well under five feet, and her muscles aren't springy.

As Alyssa and her peers matured, the players became much more skilled. Participation grew increasingly difficult for her as the level of competition increased. She doesn't run fast, kick hard, or throw far. Nor does she possess competitive enthusiasm in athletics. Sports stopped being fun for her.

After much vacillating, I accepted inclusion in sports was not in Alyssa's best interests. To be sure, she needed physical activity and social interaction, but not in a highly competitive venue. I investigated Special Olympics. In the past, segregated sports had seemed like a concession—giving up on the vision we had laid out. As I learned more about the Special Olympics philosophy, I realized I was very wrong. Special Olympics provides sports competitions at all levels in an atmosphere welcoming everyone, regardless of ability or disability. Each athlete strives for their best in an atmosphere of inclusion. Yes, there's inclusion in Special Olympics. Athletes and coaches come together to find joy in practice and competition, forming a uniquely bonded community.

Alyssa first joined Special Olympics bowling. She practiced weekly with a small group of athletes, and they became friends. Next, our county set up cheerleading and basketball programs. Cheering fit her because of her dance background. Basketball—not so much, but she enjoyed cheering for her fellow athletes at the basketball games.

I remember the first time Alyssa went to a regional competition with Special Olympics. I was guarded. Watchful. I often assume this role when she participates in activities with her typical peers. I observe to make sure she engages appropriately. Are her words or actions causing a problem? Does she understand what she's doing? Is she fitting in? Should I intervene? This time, though, I could lower my radar. Though some athletes competed fiercely, the overall atmosphere fostered cooperation and friendship. We did not need to conform to a system catering to a particular norm. Each person competed to the best of their ability and took pride in achievement. I felt free. I imagine Alyssa experienced incredible release from the pressure to perform she found in typical sports.

Despite my initial reluctance, Special Olympics was the right choice for Alyssa. She gained competence in many sports. In soccer and floor hockey, she prefers individual skills to competitive team play. In softball, she always asks to be the pitcher. She prefers not to participate in walking and running competitions. She swims like a dolphin underwater, or maybe she'd rather characterize herself as a mermaid. She'd love to do cheering again, but our current state doesn't offer this program. She's super-enthused about basketball skills, though she cannot yet shoot the ball through the net. All in all, bowling remains her all-time favorite sport.

Special Olympics gave Alyssa the opportunity to explore a variety of athletics. She has a great way to stay active and healthy. More importantly, she benefits from friendship and acceptance. She delights in a fun place where her abilities are celebrated.

I too found fellowship in the Special Olympics family. As a coach for various sports, I have the privilege to get to know athletes from all walks of life. Additionally,

I count many of the parents and fellow volunteers as friends. These diverse individuals bond over athletics, but the community doesn't stop there. To enhance these relationships, our program also organizes social activities throughout the year.

I almost missed out on a staple of our life. Years ago, I had formed a plan—a good, working plan. In the meantime, life happened. Alyssa showed us her needs strayed from my course. Though God provided a new opportunity for her through Special Olympics, I resisted. My mind was closed. Did I mention I'm often stubborn?

Because of love for Alyssa, I flexed my will to adjust to her needs and consider a new—and better—thing provided by God to meet our needs.

EVER PRESENT

Do not fear, for I am with you; do not be afraid, for I am your God. I will strengthen you, I will also help you, I will also uphold you with My righteous right hand. (Isaiah 41:10)

Alyssa was changing. Surging anxiety. Abnormal fear of strangers. Insatiable appetite. Spending an inordinate amount of time in the bathroom getting ready for the day. She dug in her heels more than usual at times of transition and change in routine. Seeking control, she argued every point. Occasional spells of fainting drove us from doctor to doctor seeking a diagnosis. We thought she might be having seizures, but tests ruled out the possibility. I couldn't understand what was happening. In desperation, I cried out to God.

A year or so had passed before I reached this breaking point. At first, I assumed our recent move from North Carolina to Kentucky had taken its toll on Alyssa. The relocation had been rough. At the old house, a serious water leak, a broken sales contract, and chicken pox during the selling process stretched our nerves like an old, brittle rubber band. I shook the dust and problems of the old house off my feet when at last, the time came for me and the kids to join Jeff in Kentucky. Setting up our new home, though, presented even more challenges. A delay in the closing, a moving truck full of household goods, and essential repairs twanged already taut emotions.

I allowed Alyssa's condition to slide for a while. I unpacked the boxes. Settled into the house. Reestablished our homeschool routines. We joined an active co-op group. Our search for a church took longer, but we found a new place of fellowship. I figured we would all relax as life resumed some normalcy.

Alyssa did not return to normal as we settled in. Her behaviors changed. In the past, food held little interest for her. She was picky with only a few favorites. Now, she was raiding the refrigerator at night. Always a sound sleeper, dreams disrupted her rest. The daily news and movies frightened her. Thoughts and events replayed in her mind, the repeated themes leaking out into conversations and writing. She created endless, useless lists. I acknowledged we needed intervention the day I found my previously friendly and outgoing girl cowering in her room because a repair man had come into the house to fix our dishwasher.

I wish I could say knowing there was a problem paved the way to a quick solution, but I continued to flounder in confusion and worry.

In the winter, I heard about the National Down Syndrome Congress annual convention in Kansas City. Many years earlier, we had attended one of their conferences, so I yearned for the encouragement I knew I would find there. For a family of four, though, the price was prohibitive. Our household budget barely balanced after a lengthy layoff from work precipitated our move to Kentucky for a new job. I heard about a state grant I might be able to use to cover some of the costs. I completed what seemed like a ream of required papers and sent off the application, hoping for a miracle. A few weeks later, God provided the funding to send us.

As the following July's convention date approached, Alyssa's symptoms worsened.

"Oh, God, please give me answers."

"I want to understand."

"Help me!"

I implored God every single day. Might there be a speaker or a workshop to address our unique concerns? I wasn't even sure what to look for, but I dared to hope.

We turned the drive to Missouri into a family vacation. We visited landmarks and historical sites along the way, but the lack of routine threw Alyssa out of kilter. Constant attempts to smooth over the frayed edges of her emotions exhausted me. By the time we arrived at the hotel in Kansas City, I craved rest and refreshment.

I checked in as Jeff dragged luggage and children from the car. I opened the hotel room door with a sigh and flopped on the bed, convention program in hand. Stuart planned to attend the siblings conference. Alyssa would hang with us. Anxiety prevented her from joining the other young adults in the self-advocate group. I scanned the schedule and circled anything of interest. One workshop about adults with Down syndrome caught my eye. Alyssa was a few short years away from the transition out of childhood. The title merited a big star.

On the second day of the conference, Jeff and I split up to attend different workshops. I went alone to a session led by Dr. George Capone. This popular speaker attracted a crowd to his presentation. I slipped into one of the few remaining chairs near the back. Dr. Capone, a neurologist specializing in neurobehavioral and psychiatric disorders associated with Down syndrome, spoke.

As is my nature, I scribbled notes. He explained the low incidence of mental health issues with Down syndrome and enumerated the most common symptoms. My pen dropped from suddenly slack fingers onto my notebook. Stunned, I just listened. He described my daughter as if he knew her. I stifled sobs as tears gathered in my eyes and spilled over to trickle down my cheeks. Finally, someone understood.

My mind divided—part listening and part planning—as Dr. Capone continued through the remainder of his talk. At the conclusion, I bolted to the front of the room, joining the line of people waiting to ask questions. Boy, did I have questions. First and foremost—to ask about a referral to a doctor like him in Kentucky. I swiped my damp cheeks as I approached. After some pleasantries, I dove in.

"You've described my daughter, Alyssa, perfectly." I drew a deep, shaky breath as tears threatened again. "I live in Kentucky," I said, "and I'd like to find a doctor there who can help with this." Pausing, I searched his face. "Do you know anyone?"

"I'm afraid not." At my crestfallen appearance, Dr. Capone said, "How far are you from Baltimore?"

On the spot, I made up my mind. I didn't care how far from Baltimore we lived. We'd go there. "I'll find a way to get there," I answered. "How soon can we come?"

"Use this number to call my assistant." He pressed his card into my hand. "Call when you get home, and she'll squeeze your daughter in right away."

Beaming, I pumped his hand in thanks and headed for the door. Hope coursed through my veins as I flew through throngs of attendees to the place where I had arranged to meet Jeff. As soon as he got within earshot, the words tumbled from my lips. "We're going to Baltimore. There's a doctor there who can help."

Jeff, who takes longer to come to decisions, blinked in confusion. "What are you talking about?" I reined in my excitement and relayed from the beginning what had happened. After a moment, he jumped on board.

A month later, Alyssa and I sat at Kennedy Krieger Institute in Baltimore waiting to see Dr. Capone. He delivered help and hope as he diagnosed her mental illness and prescribed medication and therapy to reduce symptoms. Putting a name—anxiety—to her condition, while distressing in some ways, provided a path out of the darkness of the unknown into the light of hope. In the years since, both of us have come to rely on his care and wisdom. He is one of Alyssa's favorite doctors, and I suspect many other patients feel likewise.

The next day, navigating up, down, and around the green mountains of Maryland, West Virginia, and Kentucky, with the sun warming my face, I had plenty of time to think. The journey to Dr. Capone via mental illness had been protracted and at times excruciating—and I'm not referring to the lengthy drive. Once again, I took an expedition I had not planned. One I had no desire to take. In fact, if I had the power, I'd change only one thing about Alyssa. I would wave my magic wand and remove the anxiety plaguing her mind.

Yet gratitude flooded my heart. God heard my cries and showered me with compassion. He stayed with me every step of the way, guiding, directing, and providing.

He still is today.

FOLLOWING

Since we are living by the Spirit, let us follow the Spirit's leading in every part of our lives. (Galatians 5:25 NLT)

"You're just like my grandma." With the heartfelt declaration, Alyssa threw her arms around the surprised silver-haired woman at the kids' Bible club.

I observed this event from across the room. In fact, I could not even hear Alyssa. I straggled behind, a human pack mule strung out between her and Stuart. As usual, my kids were not moving at the same pace. This time, Alyssa sprinted ahead while Stuart lagged. My harried thoughts, already reviewing the plan for the meeting ahead, diverted to her actions in annoyance.

What is she up to now? Alyssa's impulses often led her away from my explicit directions. *Why isn't she going to our table to get set up? She shouldn't be bothering Marci right now.*

She didn't know Marci well. Nor did I. Along with many others, we had been serving together at the Bible club for the past couple months, but we had not interacted much with Marci and her husband. A quiet soul, she kept to herself as she ministered to the children in her group. I fretted about what Alyssa might be saying. Sometimes she's a bit, let's say … unconventional. I debated how quickly

I could deposit my load and reach them to intervene. I always wonder how so many thoughts can flash through a mom's mind in an instant.

"Alyssa ..." I called from the doorway across the room, giving no hint of my inner turmoil. Sometimes, I manage to keep a calm mom facade in public. She ignored me. *Grrrrr.* I had no choice but to go to my table to drop my things before turning to investigate. By the time I took a few steps toward her, she had left Marci and returned to me.

I had no time to question her. The clock on the wall reminded me a horde of elementary-aged kids would soon arrive. We joined the team assembled in a circle to share a devotion and prayer. Announcements followed, and we dispersed to our tables to finish setting up.

The screech of air brakes outside announced the arrival of a bus full of kids. Laughter and chatter filled the room as they trooped in. Alyssa helped to lead the songs, demonstrating all the motions. She also joined in teaching the lesson whenever a scene required dramatic reenactment. When we divided into small groups, she assisted me in listening to kids' memory verses. After an hour, the bell rang, and the children rushed out in a whirlwind.

By then, Alyssa had reached her limit of human interaction, so she retreated to a quiet place with a book while the team wrapped up. I was busy stashing my materials to leave when I heard a throat clear behind me. I turned to find Marci.

"Your daughter really blessed me today," she said in her soft voice. A slight smile tipped the corners of her mouth.

"What do you mean?" Apprehensive, I wondered what I might need to explain about Alyssa. Sometimes people use the word blessed but don't mean it.

Marci related the event I had witnessed and not heard. "She pushed through that door …" She gestured. "… and made a beeline for me." Her grin widened. "And she called me Grandma." She recounted the bear hug Alyssa had laid on her. "It was exactly what I needed." Marci was happy with Alyssa's enthusiasm.

I relaxed.

More of Marci's unexpected story tumbled out. "I too have a daughter with Down syndrome." My jaw dropped. People who are in the same boat usually identify themselves to me early on. For reasons of her own, she had concealed our sisterhood. "She's fifty-four and living in California." She paused, looking down. "Right now, she's in the hospital."

When she looked up again, her light blue eyes filled with tears. The words poured out in choked fits like a faucet turning on and off. Her daughter was critically ill. Marci scrambled from afar to make good decisions not only about her current care, but also about her future placement should she survive.

Marci dabbed her cheeks with a tissue as she struggled to stem the tide of her emotions. I was crying too. What could I say? Though Alyssa was still young, the problem of aging had already crossed my mind. Sometimes, the worry tarried there. Often, we have no good answers. I embraced Marci and wept with her.

God had used Alyssa as a vessel of His love and encouragement. How did she know what Marci needed? She didn't, but when the Spirit inside her prompted, she responded. I doubt she paused even for a moment to second-guess before she acted.

I've seen her special connection to God's Spirit before. When she was about ten years old, we were walking in our neighborhood and a woman with a baby in a stroller approached. I murmured a greeting and moved past, but Alyssa stopped dead in her tracks, saying she'd like to pray for the child. The young mom welcomed the intercession.

Another time as a teen, she volunteered at the YMCA folding towels. A middle-aged man came to the reception desk asking about membership. Alyssa, working nearby, overheard him explaining he had recently moved to the area. "You need to go to church," she said.

Startled, the gentleman swiveled her way. "I think you're right," he answered. "But I'm not sure how you knew I've been looking." She shrugged and invited him to our church.

Or another time, Alyssa made a card for her grandma, who faced a dire medical diagnosis. Unaware of the serious nature of the condition, she copied a Bible verse about courage to go with her own words of support. "I needed to hear those words today," my mom said through tears.

These moments happen only every now and then. I can't explain how it all works, but each time, I marvel at God's use of Alyssa's willing heart.

I must admit, though, sometimes I'm so impatient I almost interfere with the Spirit's work through her. Often my timing and God's timing differ. I confess Alyssa sometimes throws me out of my comfort zone when she yields to the Spirit. I don't like to feel conspicuous and out of control.

God is gracious. He counteracts my attitude issues with abundant longsuffering. He shows me, time and again, how well he knows her. After all, she's his child first. He created her so she could know his voice and walk in step with his Spirit.

Though I've taught Alyssa many things about God over the years, she teaches me even more by her example of following the Spirit's leading.

HEAVEN PLUS

And my God will supply all your needs according to His riches in glory in Christ Jesus. Now to our God and Father be the glory forever and ever. Amen. (Philippians 4:19–20)

"Wheeeee!"

I remember my euphoria as a kid whizzing down hills on my Schwinn bike, hair streaming behind me, both arms outstretched to the sky. My bike was the ticket to the world.

I was around five years old when my fourth brother outgrew a small-framed blue Schwinn and passed the bike down to me. I hopped up and down at the thought of joining adventures outside the yard. After mastering pedaling and balancing, I soon cruised the streets of my neighborhood. What freedom.

As a rite of passage, bike riding moves children to a new level of development and interaction with the world. On my first expedition, I biked to the pool located a couple miles away from home. I followed my brothers across a busy highway to get there. Though nowhere near safe by today's standards, we somehow all survived. As a young teen, I rode far beyond my small town. I learned to navigate in every direction without getting lost—too often. In an age where parents saw no need to cart their children to preplanned events, I provided my own transportation to socialize with friends or participate in sports. Some years later, I biked in my white Dairy Queen uniform to my first real job through sweltering sun, driving rain, and chilly evenings. After I saved a few bucks, though, the love affair with my ten-speed fizzled with the purchase of my first car.

I hoped Alyssa could enjoy at least some of the freedom and independence my bike had afforded me, so we provided wheeled opportunities from an early age. The plastic big-wheel trike came first. Low muscle tone and loose joints meant she struggled with pedaling. With the help of her physical therapist and much hard work, she got the hang of rotating the pedals. She never tooled around the driveway at breakneck speeds like her cousins, but riding thrilled her.

Because Alyssa is petite, she rode the toddler trike longer than most, but after several years, she outgrew it. Next, we found a small bike fitted with training wheels. Pedaling while sitting upright posed a bigger challenge than I anticipated. While she had learned the skill on the trike, her legs angled differently on the bike. Instead of pushing her feet out in front, she needed to press toward the ground. Also, foot placement on the pedal proved difficult. I trotted beside her, guiding the bike, shouting encouragement. "You can do it. Keep your toes on the pedals."

With all her attention riveted on the lower half of her body, Alyssa's steering wobbled and wandered. "Trot" may be too strong a word for what I was doing. Quite often, she stopped, feet fighting with spinning pedals while I held her upright. "It's too hard." she complained, frustrated. I too felt defeated.

Like so many times before, we persevered until Alyssa could control the pedals. Next, the focus turned to steering.

She also has attention deficit disorder, so anything can swivel her neck and mind. A dog's bark, the blowing breeze, a car passing by, or a leaf skittering across the path can upset her. Literally. You expect the training wheels to prevent spills, but we learned otherwise. Scrapes and bumps became badges of honor as she kept trying.

A long spring and summer of perseverance passed. The time to ditch the training wheels came, and progress screeched to a halt. Though she had achieved first pedaling and steering, balancing was the end of the bike lane. Alyssa could not combine all three skills. Though we tried again several times in her teen years, we accepted the death of the dream.

A few years later, the entire family attended a Down syndrome convention, as we try to do every so often to encourage and inspire ourselves on this journey. We always visit the giant hall where hundreds of vendors peddle their specialized wares and services. Jeff and I were browsing the booths and taking notes amid chattering crowds when we turned the corner and bumped into a large display of bikes. Well, to be more exact, trikes. The sellers were demonstrating the trikes, which they customized for the needs of individuals with Down syndrome. We saw a young man who had never ridden a bike climb aboard. After the expert fiddled with sizing and added modifications, the novice negotiated the short figure-eight track on the floor like a pro.

My biking dream for Alyssa instantly resurrected. Because trikes eliminate the need for balance, we had considered them before, but sizing was always a barrier. This company, though, said they could fit one to her stature. Later in the day, right after Alyssa's convention session ended, the three of us hustled back to the bike booth.

While we waited our turn, she peered around the taller people blocking her view. Her excitement mirrored my own.

"Are you ready to try, young lady?" the sales rep asked. He measured her with his eyes and made some adjustments to the seat and handlebar.

"I'm ready." Without hesitation, Alyssa hopped onto the gleaming red machine. The gentleman helped put her feet into cups fixed to the pedal to hold them in place. He also replaced the traditional handlebars with a triangular steering wheel. "Yee-haw!" She was raring to go.

Oohs and aahs rose from spectators around us and resonated in our hearts as Alyssa glided on the bike. Some claps even broke out as she negotiated every turn. She has always loved an audience. Her huge grin and sparkling eyes settled the matter. We were sold.

I saw no prices in the product brochure, a sure sign of an expensive price tag. This trike would be beyond our budget, yet we approached the rep with hope. Perhaps we could get a grant?

What happened next left my heart overflowing.

"Your daughter's a natural," the rep said.

"Yeah, we'd love to see her be able to ride around our neighborhood."

He noticed Jeff's Air Force ball cap. "Are you a veteran?"

"Yep. Twenty-two years in the Air Force," Jeff answered.

"I know some veteran groups who help fund these trikes." The announcement piqued my excitement. "With your permission, I'll write out a proposal." The rep whipped out a tape measure and noted the length of Alyssa's arms and legs. We discussed various modifications.

"All done," he said, sliding the measure back into his pocket. "We'll contact a group in your area and be in touch when we find funding."

We floated on air back to our hotel room. We had not gone to the convention looking for a bike. We had not ever asked God for this gift. Yet, out of his infinite riches, he blessed us. As a good friend often quips, "There's all this—and heaven too."

Several months later, veterans at a local VFW surrounded us as they presented Alyssa with her new trike. Beaming, she thanked them with a colorful handmade card.

The next day, though not on a hill, Alyssa whizzed down the street, hair streaming behind her, hands gripping the wheel, heart outstretched to the sky.

"Wheeeeee!"

CHEERING SECTION

Therefore, since we are surrounded by such a huge crowd
of witnesses to the life of faith, let us strip off every
weight that slows us down, especially the sin that so
easily trips us up. And let us run with endurance the
race God has set before us. (Hebrews 12:1 NLT)

The din reached our ears long before we exited the
open gymnasium doors on our way out to the waiting
buses.

"Way to go!"

"You guys are awesome!"

"Keep up the good work!"

We were deep into a line of thousands of Special
Olympics athletes and coaches plodding out the doors into
the clear night after the assembly completed. When our
group emerged, the overhead lights revealed the source
of the now deafening noise. Villanova students, everyone
on campus, I thought, turned out to greet and cheer the
athletes. A double line of fresh-faced, red-cheeked kids
snaked along the blocks from the gym to the parking lot.
Their breath hung on the brisk night air as their already
hoarse voices whooped and hollered encouragement.
They slapped endless high fives with every excited athlete
who ran the gauntlet between them.

Some athletes, energized up by the exuberance, trotted right through the line. Others hesitated, eyes big and round. All paces are okay at Special Olympics. When Alyssa caught her first glimpse of the hubbub waiting outside the doors, she froze, overwhelmed, trying to take it all in. Others in our group knew what was coming and surged forward, but this was her first Villanova Fall Festival experience. After a moment of surveying the scene, she moved into the crowd. Pure sensory overload could not dampen the irresistible fun.

Alyssa reveled in the attention. With a broad smile dimpling her left cheek, she threw up her hands, clapping and cheering with the students. She paused often to whack the hands raised for high fives, lingering a bit longer for every handsome young guy. Others in our delegation passed by us, and I stressed as we fell behind. I urged her to walk faster, but our county leader chided me. "It's no big deal. Let her enjoy it."

So I did. I cheered and laughed and thanked the students all the way to our coach bus stationed way out in Timbuktu. Our exhausting day had begun well before dawn, but the students' joy rallied my flagging energy. The pain of aching feet and frozen hands receded as I focused on the moment.

Villanova University students have organized and implemented Fall Festival for over thirty years. Every November, they open their campus located outside Philadelphia to host the weekend sports competition for Special Olympics. The event encompasses so much more than athletics, including ceremonies, entertainment, health screenings, a street carnival, food, music, and dancing. This extravaganza is the largest annual student-run Special Olympics event in the world.

We arrived in the morning after several hours on the road. Without stopping first at our hotel, eager athletes trooped off the bus carrying their gear and identical red backpacks stuffed with uniforms they would need for the weekend. Each sport's coach gathered their athletes like a mother hen and led their trailing chicks to the location of their events. Alyssa and I set out with the soccer skills team, arriving at the fields set up between the backdrop of the stately stone halls of education and a busy road. A grove of trees, already robbed of most of their colorful fall leaves, stretched gnarled fingers through a deep blue cloudless sky, grasping at the warmth of the sun. A sharp wind snapped a flag above us and bit through our jackets as we huddled together waiting for Coach Chris to check in.

Villanova students garbed in identical, pale-yellow T-shirts soon approached and introduced themselves as Franklin County's local program hosts (LPH). Each LPH must apply and be interviewed in a careful selection process before they are approved for the job as liaison between Villanova and the county Special Olympics programs. They get to know the athletes and coaches, support them during competitions, and set a positive, enthusiastic tone for the weekend. Our LPHs waved colorful posters they had designed for our team. I surveyed the scene with gratitude as they engaged each athlete and cheered them on to do their best. Over the course of the weekend, they would often hang out with us, remembering every individual by name.

Later in the day after competition concluded, we went to Olympic Town. I had heard tales of this huge carnival, but the descriptions left me unprepared for its magnitude. Wall-to-wall people enjoyed games, music, and crafts at booths situated along the entire central concourse running between the campus buildings. Villanova student groups created activities to make O-Town fun for everyone. Music blared across the campus beckoning participants to join the dancing centered in front of the hall at one end.

Alyssa danced from one end of O-Town to the other. We stopped along the way to make crafts and color papers. She petted and whispered to guide dogs in training. She stood in the long line for her turn at karaoke, belting out a sad country song about drinking whiskey I had never heard before. I blame her father, who'd passed on his country music affinity to her. The Star Wars characters wandering around the crowd held little interest for her, but she liked meeting the handsome football and basketball players dressed in their uniforms. These giant young men dwarfed her as she cozied up for pictures with them. Afterward, we made our way to the end where a mass of dancers gyrated and sang along to songs spun by a disc jockey. Alyssa dove into the melee, swaying and twirling with friends and Villanova students. I stood on the periphery, hoping to spot her to snap some pictures. I wasn't too worried about losing her there. I figured as long as they played music, she'd be dancing.

The weekend consisted of more sports, opening, closing, and award ceremonies, pizza parties, Philly pretzels, and yes, more dancing. Late nights and early mornings drained us, but the continual presence and excitement of the Villanova students buoyed our spirits and overcame the fatigue. At the end of every day, they formed what seemed like a mile-long cheer line to honor and celebrate our athletes who, by the world's standards, seem insignificant.

Surrounded by snoring athletes on the bus ride back home late Sunday afternoon, I absentmindedly grinned at the one person who likes to take awkward sleeping pictures for social media. My mind wandered back over the events of the weekend. The positive, friendly attitude of the Villanova students impressed me. They had planned and worked for the entire year to make Fall Fest special for our athletes.

Their presence and diligence reminded me we always have an invisible cloud of witnesses, always urging us to persevere in life. We'll see them in heaven one day. Imagine if their presence and encouragement were as palpable as the students' presence at Villanova. I wouldn't be thinking about the struggles. I wouldn't be tempted to give up. I would forget the past and press on with a fresh blast of stamina toward the finish line.

Here on earth, I thank God I get to tag along with Alyssa to Villanova for this glimpse of heaven.

WHAT IF ...?

Now all glory to God, who is able, through his mighty power at work within us, to accomplish infinitely more than we might ask or think. (Ephesians 3:20 NLT)

No way!

I confess. The disbelief sprang into my mind when my friend Judy said, "What if ...?" over lunch one summer day. She suggested taking Alyssa on a mission trip to Siberia. Yes, Siberia. Though she was twenty-three at the time, I couldn't begin to fathom how to make such a proposition work.

I had been going to Siberia for years with a team of devoted Christians to share the love and kindness of God with humanitarian aid and the gospel message to the people of Russia. It is nothing short of miraculous I had already returned to Siberia nine times. The trip alone—traveling by van, planes, and train across twelve time zones to the other side of the world in February—is grueling. Sleep-deprived, the team begins the work of assembling about fifteen hundred gift packs immediately upon arrival. Every day thereafter, we spend long hours careening on icy roads in subzero temperatures to remote villages and cities visiting orphans, the elderly, the addicted, and others in need. While the work feeds my spirit, I'm physically and emotionally drained by the end. I couldn't imagine its toll on Alyssa. I doubted I would have the extra strength needed to support her there.

Once the idea pricked my imagination, though, I couldn't dismiss it. I prayed as my mind toyed with the possibilities. What strengths and needs did Alyssa bring to the mission? What accommodations could we make? What supports were available to create success? How could God use her to share his love in Siberia? Answers, ideas, and questions flooded my mind and my tablet.

My girl is Jesus-loving, smart, verbal, strong-willed, persevering, and quirky—all wrapped up in a petite package resembling a ten-year-old. She spends a lot of time thinking about her own needs. Repetitive thoughts often interfere with her enjoyment of life. Sometimes, though, I witness moments when she zeros in on unspoken needs of others with a supernatural ability straight from God. Because she is impulsive, she never holds back when the Spirit moves her. I sensed God could use those qualities in a mighty way to minister to people in Siberia.

As I got the green light from God to move ahead, I gathered a team to support Alyssa throughout the mission trip. There were four of us, and each had an assignment. Judy roomed with her. Tunnie guided Alyssa in small-group interactions. Andrea, the closest to her age, was her travel buddy. I filled in all the gaps.

Part of the process of going to Siberia is telling others about the opportunity. I encouraged Alyssa to write a letter to friends to ask for needed prayer and financial support. She wrote, "I wonder if there are people with Down syndrome in Russia who I will meet. I wonder what other people will think of me and what questions they will ask me. When they see I have Down syndrome, they will think I'm not capable of doing mission work. I hope I can use my disability to share God's Word with them and tell them how God has saved me."

God confirmed this desire in her by providing all she needed to go to Siberia.

We spent many hours in preparation and practice before the trip. We discussed the routine, looked at pictures from previous trips, learned how to use an interpreter, reviewed songs and the gospel message, and myriad other details. This preparation was essential, but I wondered how she would handle the inevitable events we could not anticipate.

The trip was fraught with opportunities to be flexible—a nice way of saying nothing went as planned. After a blizzard in New York City left us stranded there for two days, obstacles continued to derail our plans. Alyssa rarely tolerates changes from routine, but by God's grace, she handled many surprises like a pro.

Seeing God shine through Alyssa in Siberia made my heart burst with joy. She participated with the team as we created smiles and laughter for kids and adults alike. She performed in skits, played Duck, Duck, Goose, and sang songs, even in Russian. She shared her life in pictures with curious new friends, and using a multi-colored bead bracelet, she told the good news of Jesus.

I saw her shine brightest in spontaneous interactions. God's Spirit drew her to those who needed a touch, a bear hug, a smile. One day, we visited a school for young, deaf children. While the rest of the team stressed over the struggle of translations between three languages— English, Russian, and sign, Alyssa greeted and loved on the children. In elder institutions where sights and smells are shocking, she moved in with confidence and held hands, talking and smiling with the bedridden. She didn't need interpretation. She communicated heart to heart.

The response of the Russian people to Alyssa enlightened me and our entire team. Russian culture does not value people with disabilities. Parents, overwhelmed by shame and disappointment, usually consign their babies born with disabilities to life in orphanages because no one holds positive expectations for them.

Eyes widened and whispers swept through the crowd when vivacious and capable Alyssa showed up all the way from America to visit them. One of our visits happened to be to families and children with disabilities. These families had made the unusual decision to keep and raise their children with almost no support and understanding from their community. Meeting Alyssa amazed and encouraged them. Regardless of where we went, the surprise of the Russian people drew them to her message of Christ's love. In God's hands, her disability transformed to an asset.

In her letter, Alyssa also wrote, "I think God is using me and my team as gifts for people in Russia. He himself will be there with us. When we give to people, it is not for us to be thanked. It is only for God's glory."

God calls the most unlikely people to accomplish his mission. All we need is a what if? attitude and a willing heart.

UN-EXPECTATIONS

She is clothed with strength and dignity, and she laughs without fear of the future. (Proverbs 31:25 NLT)

Sometimes, I feel like throwing a tantrum. Feet stomping, fists balled, face screwed up, screaming for what I want. For what I deserve. Or at least, what I think I deserve.

Expectations can be difficult. On Alyssa's birthday, I didn't realize the laundry list of expectations I had pinned to my tiny, swaddled bundle of baby. She was my first, so I couldn't understand the hidden hopes and dreams harbored deep in the heart of every parent.

Think about your own hopes. We expect health—ten fingers and ten toes. How often have you heard someone say, "I don't care if my baby's a boy or girl, I just want them to be healthy"? When we finally cradle them in our arms, we scrutinize their miniature features, searching for a resemblance to ourselves. We look forward to normal childhood milestones—crawling, walking, talking, growing, playing sports, learning. We never doubt our child will go to school and graduate one day, perhaps even going on to college. Our innate parental pride swells with what we presume will be accomplished. Sometime later, though unimaginable at birth, we accept our child will leave home and begin life on their own one day. By the time they're teens, we may look forward to an empty nest and hope they marry and produce grandkids. At some level, we even expect our child to help care for us in our far-off old age.

We realize all children require sacrifice, but we subconsciously think a time should come when the sacrifice rewards us with a payoff. As children become more independent, we assume they will provide increasing amounts of self-care. We want some me time. We also long for our children to love and honor us.

No one ever voices these expectations when they're anticipating a birth. Nevertheless, they burrow down under our consciousness, creeping toward the surface over time.

A few years after I had Alyssa, I read a metaphor essay, "Welcome to Holland," by Emily Perl Kingsley. The author compares the experience of having a baby with a disability to planning a wonderful vacation to Italy. You buy guidebooks, learn the language, and make plans to visit the amazing sights. The preparation builds excitement. When your plane lands, however, you hear the flight attendant say, "Welcome to Holland." The natural response is extreme disappointment.

Many parents have told me of the disappointment and yes, even grief, they experienced at the birth of their child born with a disability. Their grief does not imply a lack of love but a sharp realization of lost expectations. I did not experience this emotion at Alyssa's birth, probably because I was so thankful to have a living child after such a traumatic delivery. But grief recurs as different seasons of life bring new awareness of adjustments we must make to expectations. Every time it resurfaces, we must once again relinquish a dream and embrace a new reality.

Over time, I adjusted many expectations to fit reality. I did not understand reaching every milestone would be a battle. When Stuart joined the family seven years later, I realized God designed most babies to give subtle feedback through sounds and eye contact to increase bonding. Alyssa rarely provided these responses. I also marveled at how my son slipped from one developmental level to the next. I didn't prod his tummy to stimulate muscles for crawling. We didn't teach him to pull up to cruise along the sofa. I never demonstrated how cupboard doors open to reveal the wonders of pots and pans. I couldn't imagine ever hoping for a child to be quiet after all the work I had invested in teaching Alyssa to speak.

Alyssa's friendships provoked another new reality. We all desire friends for our children. Kids figure out social norms early in life by modeling those around them. Despite occasional stumbling blocks, most seem to make connections. Alyssa's relationships, however, required facilitation from me because of delays in cooperative play and recognition of social cues. Kids usually navigate peer interaction without much assistance as they grow, and parents step back into the role of advisers. I will always be more involved.

I've also gradually released the dream of Alyssa's independence. I assumed early on I would always play a more active parental part in her adulthood, but I hoped and planned for semi-independence. As those days approached, though, we understood more about her struggle with mental illness. Her diagnosis forced us to begin the long, slow process of accepting our nest will never be empty. Now, I'm living out a different dream as a mom whose job continues. As friends are moving into a season of freedom from parental responsibility to pursue other interests, I rarely spend time without Alyssa. When meeting with friends, I almost always have a companion. Date nights alone with Jeff are a rare treat while extended getaways are nearly impossible.

Grandchildren weren't on my mind when the only evidence of Alyssa was my swelling belly, but I believe we all take this legacy of parenting for granted. When she was young, I read women with Down syndrome were unlikely to have a child. Only then did I perceive my buried desire to one day be called Grandma. At the time, she was my only child, and the sadness of loss impacted me like a blow to the head from a prize fighter. Later, acceptance brought peace to my heart, though grief resurfaces from time to time when I see friends enjoying the blessing of grandchildren.

I've provided only a few examples of my foot-stomping tantrum moments in life. I foolishly believed I deserved to have all my expectations met. As Alyssa grew, though, God revealed to me an awareness of my limited vision and control over life. All parents need to adjust expectations to varying degrees as their children mature. None of us merits a particular outcome.

Have you ever noticed how fear often skyrockets with loss of control and changing circumstances? God uses these experiences to teach me about worry. Though I prepare as best I can, I know anything could happen. What if I become unable to care for Alyssa? Where will she live? Who will protect her? What about the disconcerting statistics on dementia and Down syndrome? If I throw up my hands and release the reins on life, unbelievable anxiety surfaces in a world with surprises around every corner. When I hand the reins to God, though, peace rules my heart. Why? God knows and controls all things. He also wants the best for me. I depend on his character and love to calm my frantic outbursts.

Kingsley's essay concludes with an observation about Holland. When you settle down and stop looking for Italy, you notice your new destination has interesting scenery.

Though life with Alyssa is different than I expected all those years ago, I would not trade it. My life is richer because of her. God continues to use the unexpected to reveal new, breathtaking facets of beauty and joy.

CERTIFIED PUPPY LOVE

*He will yet fill your mouth with laughter, and your lips
with joyful shouting. (Job 8:21)*

"Go get it, Misha. Get it!" Girlish giggles pealed in
sheer joy as an inky, woolly beast with long slender legs
dashed across the living room chasing a wildly bouncing
ball. What power the simple sound held for me. I could
not remember the last time I had heard Alyssa laugh from
the inside out.

Misha, our gangly, fifty-pound labradoodle, is more
standard poodle than lab. He came to us as a pup after we
took a few years' hiatus from pets. Prior to him, we had
many furry friends, running the gamut from the usual cats
and dogs to numerous types of rodents and even exotic
chinchillas. While we enjoyed those times, we decided
to remain pet-free after our most recent girl, Cocoa, died
from old age. With our many activities, we thought life
would be easier untethered from the responsibilities of
pet ownership.

Alyssa changed my resolve against a new pet. Anxiety,
anger, and pain had plagued her for many years due to
mistreatment deep in her past, and she could not relax
her guard and open her heart. Her counselor advised me
she would benefit from the help of a service dog. Alyssa
agreed and lobbied every day for a dog to join the family.

Through extensive research, I learned it is difficult to evaluate the temperament of a very young pup. Nevertheless, I went to a breeder's home to visit her four-week-old litter. Most people look for the cutest face or sweetest personality, but I came with a different agenda. My puppy had to have a boldness coming slightly shy of being impetuous. He needed to be tolerant of handling, pinching, and pulling. A strong drive to eat was a huge plus. Most young pups do not possess these qualities. One by one, I handled all eleven puppies and put them through the paces. Their varied responses surprised me. I was a novice, so I begged God to help me select the right puppy for Alyssa.

Of course, all the puppies were adorable. Some were all chocolate, some were all black, and some were both colors mixed with white. One stood out from the rest—a miniature mass of coal black curls with a tiny spot of white on his back left toe. Barely into the weaning process, he stood out as the only puppy who would chase a meaty treat. When I placed him on a slippery hardwood floor for the first time in his life, he scrambled to investigate the shoes lined against the wall. The other pups stood, legs splayed, frozen in fright. This one startled to noise but recovered to investigate its source. Best of all, he accepted handling and snuggling like a pro. He was the one.

We sifted through names to link with his tiny, button-nosed face. Because of our connection to Siberia, I knew Russians name their teddy bears Misha (short for Michael). Our adorable boy resembled a cuddly teddy bear, so we dubbed him Misha.

When Alyssa met Misha a few weeks later for the first time, my heart melted. She didn't quite know how to respond to the wriggling, nosing bundle of curls, but Misha knew what to do. He wormed his way into her lap and deep into her heart.

Misha joined his puppy training class at twelve weeks. "Will work for food" was Misha's motto, so he picked up many basic commands in exchange for tidbits of meat. Next in the training process was public access. In this phase, we exposed him to numerous environments and people to acclimate him to handle any situation without much reaction. Additional training helped Misha to learn impulse control. We used toys, food, small children, other animals, flapping flags, noises, and scents to tempt young Misha to break from service protocol.

The final step of training was learning tasks. Any would-be service dog must learn specific jobs customized to a particular individual's needs. Misha, an excellent canine student, performed commands to retrieve, open, close, pull, and put things in place. Alyssa's needs were more psychological than physical, so I taught Misha to detect and respond to signs of anxiety. He learned to lie upon her lap and to lick on command. He also pressed in close to her body and used his large moist nose to interrupt self-harming behaviors.

Misha has a special something that is more than training. He possesses an innate ability to sense Alyssa's emotional needs. To us, they are complex. For him—simple. When she's in a funk, he brings his Kong toy to her and won't take no for an answer. Though much too big to be a lap dog, Misha sprawls across her, anticipating her caress when she talks to her therapist about tough memories. Every night at bedtime, Misha lies with her to say prayers and tuck her in. His puppy love is a powerful force.

Alyssa loves her Misha. We've had many pets over the years, but he is the first to capture her whole heart. She claims her role as his mother and calls me his grandmama. Besides being attentive to his need for food and water, she spends time every day "getting his ya-yas out," as she likes to say. Though usually a serious soul, she will engage in playful baby puppy talk with Misha as she snuggles him and throws his ball. He springs off the floor on jackrabbit legs every time, twisting to catch his toy midair. Her smile comes from the heart, evidenced by the appearance of the dimple in her left cheek.

After scads of time spent in training, Misha, though quite smart, revealed a fatal flaw—barking at canine friends. Though barking disqualifies him from certification as a service dog, Misha's bond with Alyssa touches my heart. The countless hours and too much money spent training and caring for Misha were well worth hearing my sweet girl's genuine laughter again. God used this simple dog to release an unguarded, free side of Alyssa, which she had hidden for many years.

Though Misha will never be a certified service dog, he is already one hundred percent certified in our hearts.

ALYSSA-ISMS—KEEPING IT REAL

Therefore I, the prisoner of the Lord, urge you to walk in
a manner worthy of the calling with which you have been
called, with all humility and gentleness, with patience,
bearing with one another in love. (Ephesians 4:1–2)

The spectacle was over in the blink of an eye, yet it
dragged on for eternity. I watched from afar, like gaping at a
car crashing on the highway ahead, impotent to intervene.

I had settled on my swivel chair in the spectator row at
the bowling alley, relaxing a bit and taking a break from
the coaching paperwork I was notating. Sights and sounds
assailed my senses, reassuring me all was well with my
sixty athletes. The *thunk* of urethane balls dropped on
glossy maple lanes. Whirring, colorful spheres spinning
toward the yawning pin deck. The crash of toppled
wooden soldiers. An occasional kerplunk into the gutter.
Laughter, groans, and cheers.

My eyes roamed the lanes pausing on Alex. His round,
furry belly peeped out from under his T-shirt. This sight
was nothing new. What caught my attention was the
dangerously low level of his sweatpants. When he bent
over to retrieve his ball from the return, I groaned. There
it was. The plumber's crack. The crescent moon. The place
where the sun don't shine.

I've always claimed Alyssa says, and sometimes does, what others are thinking. This time, she went all the way. As I sat dumbfounded, she marched over to Alex in the next lane. Face level with his bulging abdomen, she grasped both sides of the waistband of his stretchy pants and yanked. Hard. The pants now covered the offending skin. "There, you look better," she said. "Keep your pants up. You don't want to be immodest." With a final satisfied glance, she wheeled about, returned to her group, and sent her ball meandering down the lane.

The pants police had struck. Alex stood frozen, slack-jawed with eyes as big as dinner plates. He turned to the other athletes in his lane. "Did you see what that girl did?" he said, pointing at Alyssa. "She pulled my pants up." Everyone shrugged, and play resumed.

I almost fell off my chair laughing. What else could I do? Scold Alyssa for touching Alex's pants? Remind Alex to keep his own pants pulled up? I chose the coward's path and reveled in the humor.

A reading specialist with a PhD once informed me Alyssa has no inner voice. Most people can say words in their heads and choose whether to repeat them out loud. Alyssa—not so much. She also has attention deficit disorder, so her thoughts—and words—fly fast and furious. This characteristic leads to many awkward, beautiful, amusing, humbling, and wishing-the-floor-would-open-and-swallow-me moments. Not all at the same time, mind you. The variety keeps me on my toes.

While I have long since forgotten most of these precious moments, I have retained some favorites.

We gathered with friends for dinner at a music club at the beach. Behind our table, a group of men talked and laughed. Alyssa turned to warn them. "Don't get too drunk. Your wives won't be happy when you're passed out in the morning."

After scarfing down a piece of cake which was to be shared with her friend Judy, she turned to her and planted a moist, chocolate kiss on her cheek. "I'm sorry." Probably not sorry enough to stop her the next time though.

A friend was chatting with an acquaintance who detailed all the woes and consequences of his addiction. "You have the demon of alcohol in you," Alyssa said to the man, a stranger to her. "I'm going to pray you get rid of it."

Another friend made the mistake of taking her into the exam room during a doctor's appointment. First, Alyssa insisted my friend receive a flu shot. She also convinced the doctor to give her a tetanus booster. My friend came out rubbing her aching arms and shaking her head. I bet you can guess who never comes in to see the doctor with me.

Jeff, Alyssa, and I were walking on the beach. I fell behind searching for whole shells and shark's teeth. Alyssa, eager to return to the hotel, said, "C'mon, Mom, you're not Dora the Explorer." I wasn't even aware she had ever watched Dora.

When we go out to a restaurant with friends or family, she always announces to everyone at the table I will be paying for all their meals. That's a bit awkward.

I was talking to the director of Good News Camp where I volunteered for a week. She mentioned they had no one to be the missionary during the last week of camp. Without missing a beat, Alyssa jumped into the conversation. "My mom's a missionary. She'll do it." Because of Alyssa, I came to spend the hottest, muggiest week of every summer teaching kids about sharing the gospel.

A visit to someone's home means she will inspect the contents of their refrigerator. Despite overt and repeated warnings from me, she always manages to walk out the door with some trophy food at the end of our time together. Food is her love language.

Alyssa's favorite refrain: "I'm serious." To which I answer, "So am I." To which she replies, "No, you're Miss Firm." The struggle to get the last word with her is real.

She is the perfect person to take to a timeshare sales presentation. I know this because I've sat through quite a few with my mother-in-law, who has a hard time saying no. Alyssa, however, has no problem with speaking up. I've never seen a sales rep release us so quickly.

I've learned never to take Alyssa car shopping. The fine art of negotiation is lost on her. At the end of a test drive for Jeff's truck, I asked about the price. Upon hearing the number, she said, "Sounds good. My dad's gonna buy it." The price haggling came to a screeching halt.

She avoids long goodbyes. When visitors linger after announcing they're going to leave, she pushes them to the door. "It's time to go." The implied message, "And don't let the door hit your backside on the way out."

Her mind captures many facts. What she doesn't know, she surmises. If you believe her, she knows all the laws of the universe, and she'll be sure to advise you if you're breaking any of them. Google helps resolve disputes.

All parents teach their kids to avoid certain impolite words, though the tolerance varies from family to family. These variations bother Alyssa. Affectionately known as the Word Police, she corrects the bad words others say. When she became an adult, I told her she could occasionally use the word butt. Her newfound freedom alleviated much of the problem.

The leader of a church youth organization recommended she not return because she warned another girl she'd go to hell if she didn't turn to Jesus. Maybe she didn't state her opinion in love, but she wasn't wrong.

"I'm a mess," a friend scolded herself when a frantic search through her purse didn't produce her lost cell phone. Without missing a beat, Alyssa said, "No, you're not a mess. You're a beautiful mess." Followed by a hug, of course.

Once we waited in a parking lot outside a restaurant for Jeff's family to join us. They drove up, and Uncle Allen got out of the car, a cigarette dangling from his lips. Alyssa made a beeline for him, snatched the "cancer stick" from his mouth, and flung it to the ground. "You don't need that." Uncle Allen barely stifled a curse, but the look on his face told us what he thought.

We live in an area where many Amish and Mennonite, plain people, reside. The women all wear similar modest dresses. At a farm market, a young, plain woman rang up our produce. Out of the blue, Alyssa said, "I love your beautiful dress." The gal's gaze jerked up in surprise from her work of bagging before she thanked Alyssa. I bet Alyssa was the first and only outsider who had complimented her clothing.

These are but a few examples of Alyssa-isms.

As parents, we experience immense pride when our children behave well in public. At those times, we imagine we're not doing too bad at the parenting thing. On the other hand, every kid has moments which tempt parents to pretend they belong to someone else. Nevertheless, I'm delighted Alyssa has a voice, though it's always on the outside. She jumps right to the heart of a matter, often crashing through some etiquette barriers.

Meanwhile, she keeps me humble.

BELIEVING IS SEEING

Now faith is the certainty of things hoped for, a proof
of things not seen. For by it the people of old gained
approval. (Hebrews 11:1–2)

A young, blonde woman at the grocery store. Bible camp.
The name Julie. How are these three things connected?

My girl can tell you. Something inside drives her to
connect. She links anything—people, movies, songs,
events, even plans. She uses this technique to make sense
of the world. I suppose the inclination to relate resides in
all of us. We seek points of connection on which to hook
relationships and understanding. Alyssa expresses this
desire in fascinating ways. Because she processes so much
by speaking aloud rather than inside her head, I have a
window into her mind, albeit a small and foggy one.

Sometimes, I find her desire for connection downright
adorable. If she feels rapport with someone, she tries to
find something in common. Often, she notices clothing
choices. "Look, we have the same color shirt," she'll say.
"We're twinsies."

Alyssa synthesizes stories using an amalgamation
of all her beloved characters from her favorite books. If
Heidi, Captain America, and the kids from Narnia are
great individually, imagine how awesome they can be
together in a story.

Alyssa knows the names of many celebrities. If someone she meets happens to have the same first name as a famous person, she assumes the person *is* the celebrity. I'll prompt her. "How many people are there in the world with the name Gretchen?"

"You're right, there are lots of people with the same name," she'll answer. "But—"

I cut her off before she comes up with some plausible reason why this could be the celebrity. "Well, this is a different Gretchen." Sometimes my assertion settles the matter. Other times, unconvinced, she launches into a discussion with a very confused noncelebrity who nods and smiles a lot.

Because time and geography aren't linear in Alyssa's brain, she can relate almost anything. We have drummed into her the concept of strangers versus friends. She knows we don't hug strangers. Ever. Unfortunately, the rule doesn't protect her when her mind is convinced she knows the person. Details may vary, but the same scenario replays over and over. We're cruising the aisles at a store. After pausing for a moment of chit-chat with a fellow shopper, I'm dismayed to see her throwing her arms around a stranger.

"You remember, we don't hug people we don't know?" I say after smiling at the bemused young woman and ushering Alyssa away.

"But she's Julie from camp when I was little," she says, reaching deep into the recesses of her past.

Sigh. I know better than to remind her of the facts. They won't be remembered the next time this happens. She hasn't been little for twenty years and those camps she attended are not anywhere near where we currently live. The possibility she knows this person is nil, but she is not deterred. The kind woman beams and hugs her back, reinforcing Alyssa's perception.

Some say every hammer sees a nail. Often, Alyssa sees what she's been fixated on. If she watches a movie over and over, her favorite actor appears everywhere—in commercial voiceovers, in other movies, on the radio. If she listens to her favorite band, she becomes convinced the lead vocalist will call and ask her to sing a solo. If she's longing for a visit from a friend and the doorbell chimes, she's sure they're standing on the other side of the door. So sure, in fact, she's wearing her shoes and coat, all ready for an adventure.

Alyssa's penchant for planning takes connecting to the next level. Her lightning quick mind navigates a path through all obstacles to her desired activity. She loves to see Nana more than anything. If I plan to visit over the weekend, she'll lobby to move the departure to an earlier day. On Wednesday, she'll wake up and push her plan.

"Let's leave for Nana today, Mom."

"We have to wait 'til Saturday. I have an appointment on Friday."

Without missing a beat, her elaborate plan spills out. "Call and reschedule your appointment for next week. I know Friday is the usual laundry day, so I'll do my laundry today instead. Then we'll put yours in, and I'll help fold. We can pick up the grocery order this afternoon, pack our clothes, and leave for Nana's as soon as Dad gets home. He can call off work for tomorrow and Friday. We'll put Misha in the crate, and Stuart can take care of him when he gets home from work. Problem solved." Those last two words said together are Alyssa's favorites. She grins, success written all over her face.

"I don't know about all that." I chuckle, always marveling at her blizzard of thoughts. I wish planning were so simple. "Sorry, but we'll have to wait until Saturday."

Later in the day, when Jeff comes home from work, she appears at the door, coat and bag in hand. "Dad's home. Let's go!"

Sigh. "I told you we won't be leaving 'til Saturday."

"Nooo," she wails. "I thought we were going." Her disappointment is genuine. She was sure her plan had connected all the dots. Her mind works in mysterious ways.

Seeing is believing. The adage is true, but Alyssa displays the opposite. Believing is seeing.

Something drives her to link all things important and pleasant, filling in all the blanks in her life, creating a secure grid. Because she has formed a plan, she maintains faith. Impossibility never occurs to her. Sometimes, her beliefs thrust us into sticky situations. I've seen her speedy narrative spin unsuspecting folks' heads in bewilderment. Even so, there's something endearing, even wise, about having her kind of faith. True faith is belief in what is unseen. If you wait until the object appears in your field of vision, you don't have faith.

I'm reminded by this quality in Alyssa I should always base my life on faith and hope in what is not yet realized, what God promises for the future. I should act with absolute certainty what he says is true and will come to pass. The strength of her belief often convinces others it's true. Shouldn't I communicate my beliefs in the same sure way to draw people into the truth about God?

Problem solved.

ALYSSA IN HER OWN WORDS

How could I conclude without inviting you to hear from Alyssa? When I decided to tell my story as her mom, I asked her to write her own story. Never at a loss for words, she got busy right away. Her perspective provides helpful context to frame the tapestry of struggles and triumphs God has woven through our lives together.

Hello. My name is Alyssa Yorty, daughter of Jeff and Annie. I am also known as Lyssa, Aly Cat, Sweet Potato, and Siberian Cupcake.

I came out of the womb as a squalling and squirming bundle of joy one March morning in 1989. A nurse swaddled me and put a cap on my head. I was put on a bed with a pink blanket with stuffed animals surrounding me. I looked like a papoose with short brown hair, hazel eyes, tiny fingers, and skinny legs. Friends and family visited me in the hospital. Then I went home wearing a soft blue bunny suit. At home, I squealed with delight when my mom gave me a bath in the sink, and I was a good sleeper. In my first year, I went on a plane ride to California, I visited family in other states, and I went on my first camping trip. I was a happy baby.

When I was a year old, we moved to Pennsylvania. There I went to preschool and later to kindergarten, first, and second grades. At school I had friends. My best friend was Rachel. I remember making Sumerian pottery with my handprint in clay. There was a class pet guinea pig I kept for my own over the summer.

I went to Sunday school every week. I really liked my teacher, Mrs. Stoudt. She gave me a special handmade book I keep to this day.

We had a German shepherd named Abby and a cat named Piper. When Abby died, Piper mourned her loss. Piper liked to snooze in my clothing drawers.

When I was five, I started riding horses. I competed in horse shows, and I have many ribbons to prove it. I also joined a singing group called Energy. I even sang solos. Once we sang the national anthem at a football game of my favorite, the Philadelphia Eagles.

We also liked to go to Hershey Park. Back when I was a baby, Mom took me on the train, holding me in her lap. When I was older, I was big enough to ride the carousel and the scrambler. I was nervous on the Sooper Dooper Looper when I was little, but now I love fast roller coasters. Hershey Park is the best.

When I was little, my cousins stayed at my house for a week every summer. We went swimming, played with Barbies, went mini golfing, watched movies, and visited grandparents. Once when I visited Grandpa, his neighbor's Dalmatian bit me. There was a little blood, and I cried. I also went to my cousins' houses in the summer. Those were the greatest summers ever.

Stuart was born when I was seven years old. He was a sweet little baby with blond hair like his nana, blue eyes like his mom, tiny hands, fair complexion, sunny disposition, and skinny chicken legs like mine. I liked to hold him and feed him milk from a bottle.

My dad got a job in North Carolina, so my family, along with our cat, moved away from Pennsylvania. I felt bereft for a while.

Soon after we got a house in North Carolina, we adopted a big black lab named Cocoa. We went to the humane society looking for a small dog, but she was so sweet with soft brown eyes. We knew she was the only one for us. Cocoa was so patient when little Stuart stood on her. At night, if I had a nightmare, Cocoa slept in my room on her pillow.

I went to school in North Carolina for a while, but later Mom homeschooled me. We had lots of friends and went to co-op together. We had fun going on field trips and having parties. My best friends were Amy and Crystal. We liked to play dress-up and Barbies.

Amy and I went to youth theater together for years. I acted in four productions. I also volunteered at the YMCA and at nursing homes. I liked to help the people at the nursing homes to play bingo. I learned more about horses with 4-H, where I competed in shows. I also took dance classes and danced in recitals. Dancing is my most favorite activity of all because it makes me happy to dance for the Lord.

One of the best birthdays was when I was fifteen, and my family and friends came to celebrate. I received a big surprise present—concert tickets. Dad took me to my first concert with Jars of Clay and Jennifer Knapp.

My family often went camping. Sometimes we went with my cousins, and it was quite an adventure. We hiked in the mountains and saw beautiful scenery and waterfalls. We often swam in a lake and played in the creek. One time after swimming we put our towels on a rack to dry by the campfire. Next thing we knew, they caught fire. They were scorched. Those are some fond memories.

I went to church and learned about God. We went to a big church where we helped a lot. I went to Sunday school. It was there we first served with Global Aid Network. My family went with our church to Pennsylvania for a mission trip every fall. I sorted clothing, packed school supplies, and made gospel bead bracelets. It's fun to serve God.

Our cat Piper grew old and died in North Carolina. It wasn't long before we got another cat. We adopted her on July fourth, so we named her Liberty Belle, or Libby for short. She had ocelot stripes and swirls. She kneaded my legs with her velvety soft paws. I always took good care of her.

Living in North Carolina was a perfect time, but I never got a southern accent.

My dad was laid off from a job and got a new job in Kentucky when I was a teen. On moving day, Libby yowled mercilessly in her kitty taxi in the car even though her buddy Cocoa was lying next to her on the seat. Stuart and I watched movies in the car through all the chaos.

We bought a brown, stone house out in the country with a little pond. Dad put a tire swing on a tree out back. We often saw deer, turtles, and foxes. My mom homeschooled me throughout high school. We participated in a co-op with friends. There I studied mythology and poetry. One of the weirdest classes was the dissection class. We cut open frogs and a sheep eye. Guh-ross! (Yes, I know there's only one syllable in gross.) I graduated after my senior year with honors. Nana and Papa came to see me. I was proud of myself.

I was busy with many activities in Kentucky. I continued to ride horses and competed in shows. I wanted to dance at church, so I talked to our friend Miss Rainey about it. She and I started a dance ministry. One time Miss Rainey hurt her toe, and I put a cold soda on it to reduce the swelling. We practiced dances and performed them at church services. I participated in Special Olympics in Kentucky. We had a big track and field event at the beginning of every summer where I earned ribbons. I especially loved bowling with friends every week throughout the year.

We visited a lot of different places in Kentucky. One of my favorites was the horse park at Keeneland. I rooted for my favorite baseball team in Lexington and even got my baseball glove autographed. We camped a lot because Kentucky has many mountains and lakes to explore. We went to Bowling Green to camp at Mammoth Cave and toured the Corvette factory. I wanted to order a pink Corvette, but it was too expensive.

A few years later we moved back to Pennsylvania because Dad got a job there. We still live there. Waynesboro is a cute little town. Libby didn't cry so much on this long drive. She was a darling.

After we settled in, life went on. Cocoa and Libby liked their new home. Soon after we moved, though, we got some new pets. Stuart's friend in Kentucky offered him a chinchilla, so we went back to get him. Somehow, we came home with three chinchillas. Their names were Andy, Barney, and Dusty. They jumped very high and ran through tubes. They were the cutest little rodents.

I joined Special Olympics and play many sports—soccer, basketball, floor hockey, track, and bowling. I also sometimes play baseball. My favorite position is pitcher. After a few years, I began to ride horses again. My favorite is a pony named Duncan. He reminds me of Sea Star from *Misty of Chincoteague*. I always give my horses treats to thank them for doing a good job.

I enjoy community activities. I went to the YMCA to swim and exercise on the machines. It made me strong. I helped with a kid's Bible club every week. I led the songs and showed the motions to the boys and girls. I also go bowling most weeks with my friends. One of my favorite activities is to volunteer at the humane society. I take care of cats and kittens and socialize them to prepare for new families.

One time I went on a mission trip all the way to Siberia. That's where I got one of my nicknames. It was icy cold there, but I went to tell people about God's love.

After much cajoling, I finally convinced my parents to get a dog. I was ecstatic when Misha came to live with us. He was so tiny and cute with lots of black curls. Then he grew and grew. Now he's tall and leggy and weighs fifty pounds. He's still black, but his muzzle is chocolate colored, like his mother, and he has a white spot on his back left foot. His fur grows fast so he needs to be shaved often. He loves me and kisses me with his rough pink tongue.

Now I work and get paid. I'm learning different skills and jobs. My supervisor says I'm doing good work. One of my favorite jobs is making boxes. I also enjoy being with my coworkers. Did I mention I get paychecks?

In my spare time, I like to sit out on my sun porch to read books and color. My favorite book series is *The Chronicles of Narnia* by C.S. Lewis. I also do puzzles on my Kindle. Sometimes I go out to eat or get ice cream. Occasionally, we go to the movies.

This is my life and I love it!

EPILOGUE

"Mom, I'm thirty-three, about to be thirty-four."

Alyssa doesn't care people stop disclosing the next year's age after passing from youth. She blurts out her years with strangers and friends alike. I love this endearing quality. Shouldn't life be that way—always trusting God has another great adventure in store for you? Believing the best is yet to come?

Like most parents, I perceive these past years to be both protracted and fleeting. Yet my time at the feet of Jesus is never complete. Sometimes I've squirmed under the Teacher's knowing guidance, but there's nowhere I'd rather be than here, learning to sit tight and trust my Father from grace-filled lessons. I glance around at those reclining with me. They were as shocked as I when their knees buckled under life's circumstances. Yet here in the dirt at the base of the cross we find sustenance, healing, and understanding. Eyes upturned, hearts open, we transform at the pace God has set for us. God speaks personally to each through experiences that are at once unique and still nothing new under the sun.

Like Alyssa, I desire to connect based on shared experiences and passions. I seek to find commonalities with others as a springboard for understanding differences. I trust you, like me, recognized your many similarities with

Alyssa. Her likes and dislikes. Her goals and dreams. Her challenges and triumphs. It turns out people with overt disabilities have much in common with those of us whose challenges are easier to disguise. Down syndrome, or any disability, for that matter, never robs a person of innate shared humanity.

I pray this account of a slice of my journey from ignorance toward blissfully trusting God encourages you to take time to find links with those in your sphere who may be different. To reach out beyond your comfort zone into the unknown to include them. To bring them into a place of belonging.

More importantly, may you be inspired to join me at the foot of the cross, dependent on God, living in blissful ignorance until he reveals a void only his wisdom can fill.

ABOUT THE AUTHOR

Annie Yorty, wife, mother, writer, and speaker, extends hope and encouragement to those living through difficult situations. God has gifted her with a variety of twists and turns in life where she's had no choice but to fully rely on his person, presence, provision, and purpose. Centered and dependent on her heavenly Advocate, Annie finds daily purpose and passion by advocating for God and others.

Annie embraced the task of advocacy after the birth of her first child, Alyssa, who has Down syndrome. For over thirty years, she has led both disability and homeschool organizations to promote understanding and acceptance for individuals with intellectual disabilities.

Annie publishes a weekly blog, *Perceive God*. She also writes devotions, blogs, Bible studies, and Christian living articles for *Today's Christian Living*, *Focus on the Family*, *Living by Design*, *The Christian Journal*, *Refresh*, and others. She is a contributor to the family section at *Crosswalk,* and her work is published in *Chicken Soup for the Soul, Room at the Table: Encouraging Stories from Special Needs Families,* and *Everyday Joy.* Annie has taught and inspired audiences across four continents from Argentina to Siberia.

A lifelong learner, Annie regularly seeks new and eclectic challenges. She gravitates toward anything crafty or creative. Sporadically, she works at learning to play the piano and ukulele. Always open to travel adventure, Annie helps organize mission teams to share God's love around the world. She wishes she had more time to read, crochet, and practice Russian. Her furry beast (aka labradoodle) would like her to spend more time teaching him new tricks.

Annie lives in Pennsylvania with her high school sweetheart/Air Force veteran husband, Jeff. They have two grown children and one still in process. (Isn't everyone, really?) Amidst the fun, challenges, and chaos, Annie encourages others to look upward with her and perceive God.

https://AnnieYorty.com